How Long Have You Been With Us?

POETS ON POETRY
Marilyn Hacker and Kazim Ali, Series Editors
Donald Hall, Founding Editor

New titles

Kazim Ali, *Resident Alien*
Bruce Bond, *Immanent Distance*
Marianne Boruch, *The Little Death of Self*
Yusef Komunyakaa, *Condition Red*
Khaled Mattawa, *How Long Have You Been With Us?*
Aaron Shurin, *The Skin of Meaning*
David Wojahn, *From the Valley of Making*

Recently published

Kazim Ali, *Orange Alert*
David Baker, *Show Me Your Environment*
Annie Finch, *The Body of Poetry*
Marilyn Hacker, *Unauthorized Voices*
Joyelle McSweeney, *The Necropastoral*
Natasha Sajé, *Windows and Doors*

Also available, collections by

Elizabeth Alexander, Meena Alexander, A. R. Ammons, John Ashbery, Robert Bly, Philip Booth, Marianne Boruch, Hayden Carruth, Amy Clampitt, Alfred Corn, Douglas Crase, Robert Creeley, Donald Davie, Thomas M. Disch, Ed Dorn, Martín Espada, Tess Gallagher, Sandra M. Gilbert, Dana Gioia, Linda Gregerson, Allen Grossman, Thom Gunn, Rachel Hadas, John Haines, Donald Hall, Joy Harjo, Robert Hayden, Edward Hirsch, Daniel Hoffman, Jonathan Holden, John Hollander, Paul Hoover, Andrew Hudgins, T. R. Hummer, Laura (Riding) Jackson, Josephine Jacobsen, Mark Jarman, Lawrence Joseph, Galway Kinnell, Kenneth Koch, John Koethe, Yusef Komunyakaa, Marilyn Krysl, Maxine Kumin, Martin Lammon (editor), Philip Larkin, David Lehman, Philip Levine, Larry Levis, John Logan, William Logan, David Mason, William Matthews, William Meredith, Jane Miller, David Mura, Carol Muske, Alice Notley, Geoffrey O'Brien, Gregory Orr, Alicia Suskin Ostriker, Ron Padgett, Marge Piercy, Grace Schulman, Anne Sexton, Karl Shapiro, Reginald Shepherd, Charles Simic, William Stafford, Anne Stevenson, Cole Swensen, May Swenson, James Tate, Richard Tillinghast, C. K. Williams, Alan Williamson, Charles Wright, James Wright, John Yau, and Stephen Yenser

Khaled Mattawa

How Long Have You Been With Us?

ESSAYS ON POETRY

UNIVERSITY OF MICHIGAN PRESS
Ann Arbor

Copyright © 2016 by Khaled Mattawa
All rights reserved

This book may not be reproduced, in whole or in part, including illustrations, in any form (beyond that copying permitted by Sections 107 and 108 of the U.S. Copyright Law and except by reviewers for the public press), without written permission from the publisher.

Published in the United States of America by the
University of Michigan Press
Manufactured in the United States of America
♾ Printed on acid-free paper

2019 2018 2017 2016   4 3 2 1

A CIP catalog record for this book is available from the British Library.

Library of Congress Cataloging-in-Publication Data

Names: Mattawa, Khaled, author.
Title: How long have you been with us? : essays on poetry / Khaled Mattawa.
Description: Ann Arbor : University of Michigan Press, 2016. | Series: Poets on poetry
Identifiers: LCCN 2016031015| ISBN 9780472053292 (paperback) | ISBN 9780472073290 (paperback) |
ISBN 9780472122424 (e-book)
Subjects: LCSH: American poetry—20th century—History and criticism. | American poetry—21st century—History and criticism. | American literature—Arab American authors—History and criticism. | English literature—Arab authors—History and criticism. | English literature—English-speaking countries. |
Arab Americans in literature. | Arabs in literature. | BISAC: POETRY / General.
Classification: LCC PS325 .M38 2016 | DDC 808.1—dc23
LC record available at https://lccn.loc.gov/2016031015

*For Marilyn, in friendship and grace;
and in memory of Srinivas Aravamudan*

Acknowledgments

"Epic Temptations: On an Unwritten Poem" appeared in *Agni*, issue 44, 1997.

"Ethnic American Writing and the Challenge of Tradition" is a lecture given at the American University in Cairo, March 2015. Parts of the lecture appeared in an essay published in *Flyway*, vol. 7, no. 2–3, 2002.

"Four Uneasy Pieces" appeared in *ALIF: A Journal of Comparative Poetics*, issue 20, 2000.

"Identity, Power, and a Prayer to Repatriation: On Translating and Writing Poetry" appeared in *The Kenyon Review Online*, September 2014.

"Meet the Poet-Stranger: Three Stories and Their Aftermath" appeared in *The Kenyon Review Online*, September 2014.

"On the Poet's Presence: Thinking Back, Thinking Forth, Thinking Darwish and Tagore" appeared in *The Kenyon Review Online*, September 2014.

"On the Road with Adonis" appeared in *Banipal*, issue 41, 2011.

"Resisting the Lapse into Monologue: On the Poetics of Bilingualism in American Poetry" appeared in *South Dakota Review*, vol. 41, no. 1–2, 2003.

"Skyping with Saadi, Channeling Li Po" appeared in *Banipal*, issue 51, 2014.

"Writing Islam in Contemporary American Poetry: On Mohja Kahf, Daniel Moore, and Agha Shahid Ali" appeared in *PMLA*, vol. 123, no. 5, fall 2008.

Contents

Meet the Poet-Stranger: Three Stories and Their Aftermath	1
Identity, Power and a Prayer to Repatriation: On Writing and Translating Poetry	25
On the Poet's Presence: Thinking Back, Thinking Forth, Thinking Darwish and Tagore	41
Resisting the Lapse into Monologue: On the Poetics of Bilingualism in American Poetry	61
Ethnic American Writing and the Challenge of Tradition	74
Writing Islam in Contemporary American Poetry: On Mohja Kahf, Daniel Moore and Agha Shahid Ali	87
Translation Impossible	97
Epic Temptations: On an Unwritten Poem	101
Four Uneasy Pieces	118
On the Road with Adonis	132
Skyping with Saadi, Channeling Li Po	135
Poems and Days (A Reader's Memoir)	138

Meet the Poet-Stranger
Three Stories and Their Aftermath

1.

As a writer starting out in the early 1990s, I wanted the company of fellow immigrants who worked in the language of their adopted homelands, chiseling away at their exile and making a home for themselves in poetry. One of my first projects while in graduate school was to collect the works of U.S.-based, foreign-born poets whose native language was not English but who wrote in it. I went on to assemble an anthology of sixty-two poets, and the list has grown longer and more varied since then.

Eventually, this interest led me to the postcolonial shelves in the library, and soon enough, I wanted to know my older siblings. I learned that the earliest likely candidates for the first serious non-English poet writing in English were poets such as Henry Louis Vivian Dorozio (1809–31) and Toru Dutt (1856–77), two Anglo-Indian prodigies who wrote against tremendous odds and died in their early twenties.

Presently, the Anglophone poetry world (including international poetry in translation) continues to expand, with more poet-strangers appearing in the capitals of the English-speaking world and with more poetry in English written and published outside of traditional realms for English-language poetry. As exemplified by Nobel laureate Derek Walcott, as well as the Syrian poet Adonis, the Jamaican poet Kamau Braithwaite, and the Iraqi poet Saadi Youssef, the postcolonial poet is a resident of the metropolis—at least for part of the time. He or she is an exile, a dual citizen, a member of an ethnic minority, a member of a sectarian group, and a cosmopolitan, all at once or in some combination. With the development of new and varied zones in which he or she can operate, the foreign poet, whether living in the metropolis or not, has a greater chance of being heard at close proximity to it. Other opportunities for the poet's presence are also opening up in unprecedented places outside the Western metropolis; one of the most elaborate literary festivals in the world now takes places in Dubai. The annual poetry festival in Medellin, Colombia, features at least sixty poets who come from all corners of the globe to be heard and viewed by audiences who turn out in the thousands every night.

Even the most "national" of poets have had to become international. With the effusion of migration and the development of multiplicities of diasporic communities, poets can remain within their nations as they hop from one capital to another. Over the past few years, the prominent Iraqi poet Mudhaffar al-Nawwab has come to the United States on several occasions to give readings to Arab diasporic communities who invited him. Like an itinerant priest of a minor religion whose population is scattered over a broad territory, Al-Nawwab interacts almost exclusively with the Arab community, and then he goes back to Damascus, where he lives in exile. With only a few of his poems translated into other languages, he is and he is not an international, postcolonial poet.

Poets may or may not be engaged by the settings in which they find themselves; their approaches to and degree of engagement have to do with their sense of their audience. The level of a poet's engagement also depends on the capacity of audiences, made up of others, to take the poet in, which is a different undertaking than simply understanding his work or its context. The issue before us here in the American poetry scene is the manner in which audiences made up of poets, readers, students, scholars, and publishers have approached and received poet-strangers. Other than the obvious admiration for the art form, what "news," to use W. C. Williams's phrase, do the poet-strangers offer, and how is their work positioned within the world of American poetry? Presenting three recent anecdotes regarding the poet-stranger's presence on the American scene, I wish to probe, in particular, the reception of the work of poets from parts of the world in which the United States has recently been engaged in some form of struggle, be it military or ideological. Examining forms of estrangement that persist in our setting now, my analysis will also explore how contemporary poet-strangers have developed interesting strategies to reach out and to undermine various forms of dissonance and compartmentalization.

Story

At a memorial evening for the poet Agha Shahid Ali in March of 2002, a celebrated American poet told a story. I hope you will pardon my attempt to restate what she said:

One year, Shahid and I were applying for jobs as poets in universities. We had been both selected as finalists for two of the best jobs. We'd talked throughout the interview process and tried to help each other. In the end, each of us was offered a job. He got the job I really wanted, and I got the job he wanted. I was upset, and when we talked on the phone after we both heard the news, he tried to console me. He said, "Don't worry, darling— they gave me the job only because they wanted a darkie."

The audience in attendance laughed, and the poet went on talking for a few more minutes about her friendship with Ali. Other authors of Shahid Ali's generation also spoke at the memorial, expressing great admiration for him as a poet and as a person. Ali was a great charmer, a wonderful cook—so went the stories. After the presentations, no one I met talked about the "darkie" story.

Story

In 2001, I completed a manuscript of selected poems of the Iraqi poet Saadi Youssef, covering five decades of his writing from 1952 to 1997. While the manuscript was being considered by several publishers, another publisher I respected contacted me and asked to see the manuscript. I received a contract a month later and signed with them. This happened shortly after 9/11, as interest in all things having to do with Iraq and the Arab and Muslim world was peaking yet again. (I should say that, to the publisher's credit, this book was not the first book by an Arab author that they had published, and the idea that the book was being published in response to a fad was out of the question.) In the fall of 2002, the publisher sent me a press kit for the book that they had developed. Here is the poem that the press decided to feature:

A Vision

This Iraq will reach
the ends of the graveyard.
It will bury its sons in open country
generation after generation,

> and it will forgive its despot.
> It will not be the Iraq
> that once held the name.
> And the larks will not sing.
> So walk—if you wish—a long time.
> And call—if you wish—on all
> the world's angels and all its demons.
> Call on the bulls of Assyria.
> Call on a westward phoenix.
> Call them
> and through the haze of phantoms
> watch for miracles to emerge
> from clouds of incense.
> (Youssef, 178)

I had chosen to translate this poem and to include it in the selection because it was one of Youssef's many meditations on his country. The poem was written in 1997. The poet imagines this pessimistic scenario while observing Iraq after twenty years of exile, seeing it choked by Saddam Hussein and suffering under brutal economic sanctions, while opposition parties in exile quibble bitterly. He senses that his country "will not be the Iraq / that once held the name," a feeling borne out of nostalgia and the exilic despair that brings about an apocalyptic vision.

Upon seeing the press kit, I contacted the publisher and demanded that the poem not be featured so prominently, as it ran the risk of insinuating that the poet held a position contrary to his declared opposition to the war that the United States was about to wage on his country. If we wanted to use this occasion to show Youssef's views on the war, as expressed in his poetry, we could have easily excerpted one of his better known poems, "America, America," in which he deplores the first American Iraq war and the suffering that the war and the sanctions caused his people. I also made it clear to the publisher that this would be inappropriate publicity as the book covered forty-five years of the poet's writing, not just the then current situation. The publisher obliged, and the publicity kit was issued with another poem that had nothing to do with the war. A few months later, as the book began to receive attention, "Vision" was reprinted in the *Los Angeles Times*. It was the only excerpt that appeared in a review of the book in *Publisher's Weekly*. And Poetry Daily, one of the most frequently visited poetry websites in the United States, reprinted the poem. The genie had gotten out of the lamp, and it was drafted into the coalition of the willing against its will.

Story

A few months ago, a well-known university on the East Coast held a reading panel that was part of a symposium on poetry and the politics of violence. The invitees were the Iraqi poet Dunya Mikhail, author of *The War Works Hard*; the poet and Iraq-war veteran Brian Turner, author of *Here, Bullet*; and me. Mikhail read several poems about her experiences during the first two Iraq wars (the Iraq-Iran war of 1981–88 and Desert Storm, 1991). She also read poems written since her migration to the United States in the late 1990s. Turner, who had opposed the war in Iraq even before it began (Turner 2009), mostly read poems relating to his service in Iraq. I read sections from a sequence addressing American militarism from a domestic angle. When the question and answer session began, members of the audience lined up at two microphones and began to ask questions. After eight questions, all addressed to Turner, the moderator paused and asked the audience if anyone had any question for Mikhail or for me. No one raised a hand.

2.

The Shahid Ali story has intrigued me since I first witnessed its telling, and I have wondered how to interpret these incidents—the story as narrated and its narration—and to fit them within Shahid Ali's tremendous achievements and the various approaches he had developed to become an influential poet-stranger.

Agha Shahid Ali is probably the best-known Anglo-Indian poet in the United States, having built a strong reputation within establishment poetry circles here before his untimely death, in December of 2001, at the age of fifty-one. Among his many achievements, Shahid Ali initiated a craze about the ghazal. In 2000, Ali edited *Ravishing DisUnities: Real Ghazals in English*, an anthology of ghazals written by poets such as W. S. Merwin and Paul Muldoon. With his own poetry highly respected and as a much-adored figure on the poetry scene, Ali was the antithesis of Breyten Breytenbach's concept of the postcolonial writer as a "guest intruder"[1] and Derek Walcott's notion of the "irascible guest"² who engages in Fanonian combat with the intellectuals at the heart of the metropolis. In this regard, Ali's case provides an excellent example of the advantages of what Homi Bhabha calls "contiguity" and "infiltration" and even "sly civility" as tools working for the postcolonial intellectual within the metropolis.

Probing the sphere Shahid Ali operated within, we will note that the metropolis has changed considerably since the days of Rabindranath Tagore's emergence as the first poet-stranger to hit Western shores and the blazing stir he caused, which quickly dimmed after his winning of the Nobel Prize in 1913. Things have changed considerably even since Derek Walcott's appearance on the American scene (first as a poet from the Caribbean in the 1960s and later as a metropolitan poet in the late 1970s). And unlike Breytenbach, who comes to the United States only for short visits with a postcolonial chip on his shoulder, Ali and diasporic poets like him have lived and worked here as resident poet-strangers.

Presently, a poet-stranger is hardly ever the only immigrant or exile of his nationality in a Northern metropolis; diasporic communities from his part of the world have grown in every metropolis he could have gone to. Now a more familiar figure, the poet-stranger bears less of the representational burden, and so his or her sense of agency can draw more on solidarity with other individuals and communities of diverse backgrounds, and much less on solitary, exilic Joycean "cunning" (*Portrait* 291).³

Within the North American context, the immigrant can and may quickly become an ethnic American. There are plenty of first-generation Americans from the poet's ethnic community among whom he can position himself or against whom he can juxtapose himself. Here, the poet would have to consider the advantages he stands to gain or lose by becoming identified as *an exile from there*, rather than *an ethnic from here*. It may be possible for him to be both and to speak from these positions alternately or in combination, and in sites where these seemingly restrictive identifications can become a larger set of concentric circles that afford the poet more room for maneuverability. Considering Ali's options in this regard, the term Kashmiri-American becomes interesting as it pertains to him. As far as I know, this ethnic designation is an ethnicity of one, since Ali is the only author identified under it. Ali gets be both a solitary exile and the sole representative of his ethnic community.

The vast majority of Ali's work addresses his life in India and Kashmir and suggests a poet-persona whose concerns are shaped by exile. Ali's most "American" book, *A Nostalgist's Map of America* (1991), includes several poems drawing on his years in Arizona and New England, and it features a sequence of poems in homage to Emily Dickinson. *Nostalgist's* was Ali's third book, appearing a few years after *The Half-Inch Himalayas* (1987), which contains poems exclusively set in India. The poems in his fourth and fifth books, *The Country without a Post Office* (1998) and *Rooms Are Never Finished* (a finalist for the National Book award in 2001), are inspired by the conflict in Kashmir and the passing of the poet's mother, who was buried there.

Perhaps the exotic aura that Shahid Ali's poet friends conveyed about him at his memorial emerges from the locale and content of his poems. Also, Ali's strong attachment to the ghazal, which became his favored and almost exclusive form toward the end of his life, signaled a strong gesture toward esthetic distinction. Here, the poet carves a place for himself within the metropolitan mainstream by choosing his native prosodic form, a form on which he is the sole expert and arbiter of its utilization in English (i.e., *real* ghazals in English). In his preface to *Ravishing DisUnities*, Shahid Ali quotes from his own ghazals to demonstrate "the real thing" (*DisUnities* 1). Collected in a separate volume titled *Call Me Ishmael Tonight*, Shahid Ali's ghazals were published two years after his passing, a posthumous magnum opus that strongly identifies him with the form.

As such, Ali's prosodic trajectory narrowed from his beginnings. His first two books were written in free verse; his third, fourth, and fifth books featured rhymed and strictly metered verse along with several ghazals; and his last book featured only ghazals. Ali's prosodic evolution moved from American free verse toward traditional forms. His ghazal is a hybrid, an Urdu form written in English; the longer he stayed in the United States, the more hybridly traditional his prosody became. The act of reclaiming the ghazal came as a reaction to what Shahid Ali saw as abuse of his native form by American poets who "had got it quite wrong, far from the letter and farther from the spirit" (*DisUnities* 1). Poets such as Adrienne Rich and Robert Bly had utilized the ghazal, but without adhering to its formal rigor, resulting in what Shahid Ali called "surrealistic exercises" (1). And so "I decided to take back the gift outright" (1), states Shahid Ali with ironic use of Robert Frost's famous inaugural poem, "The Gift Outright."

The ghazal is perhaps Ali's most consciously pan-postcolonial form and, in that sense, represents a political gesture as well as an esthetic choice. His first published ghazal was dedicated to Edward Said and borrows the phrase, "being exiled by exiles" (*The Country* 12) from Edward Said's *After the Last Sky*. Shahid Ali's poems show open sympathy for the Palestinians under Israeli occupation and for Bosnians under attack by Serb and Croat forces in the 1990s. Shahid Ali's *Rooms Are Never Finished* features a translation of "Eleven Stars over Andalusia," a long poem by Mahmoud Darwish. Said had called Shahid Ali's *The Country without a Post Office* "an extraordinary achievement" (*The Country*). Shahid Ali was known as an upstanding fellow traveler in postcolonial/diasporic circles.

Clearly, Ali was seen as an important contender capable of competing for some of the best posts and awards that the American literary and academic establishment had to offer. It would not be surprising, then, that he would wish to diffuse any anxieties that this may cause among his peers.[4] Nonetheless, taking Shahid Ali's credentials and achievements into account, what could he have meant by telling his Caucasian poet friend that he was given his post only because "they wanted a darkie"? And in telling the story at his memorial, what was Ali's friend saying about his approach toward affirmative action policies, racial representation, multiculturalism, or the diversity politics from which he might have benefited? Was she only telling the story to show how impetuous Ali was? And what might explain this impetuousness in this context?

At one level, the exchange suggests a kind of performativity marked by the poet-stranger's awareness of metropolitan desire for the exotic. The poet-stranger negotiates this aspect of his background and meets his audience, in text and in person, having developed means of addressing these expectations and apprehensions and claiming a place for himself and his poetry. The poet-stranger diffuses racial and cultural tensions by being audacious, by performing an ironic or mock acceptance of the stereotypes regarding his abilities and those of his community or race or nation.

In Ali's repetition of the accusation that he only got his job because he was a darkie, we hear a form of mimicry that exorcises menace. Perhaps by repeating uncomfortable thoughts, Ali takes them "outright" from his interlocutor's mouth, diffusing the discomfort he causes by stressing his tokenism. This is a different kind of cunning; it is not Joycean silence that grants the stranger agency but the ability to break the silence around uncomfortable and unspoken thoughts.

But what happens when that mimicry of these apprehensions is mimicked again and retold—why does the menace return intact, as evidenced by the audience's choice of nervous laughter and denial (and my own unwillingness to forget the incident). Clearly, Shahid Ali's audacious self-deprecation is meant as an antidote, and we do know that antidotes bear a taste of the poison they are meant to combat. Perhaps Ali's farcical engagement with the serious issues that surround his position in American letters is meant to polarize the assessment of his work, with the audience forced to either consider him a darkie, who was only allowed in the club to create a veneer of tolerance, or to seriously consider his work, in which we will invariably discover a set of sophisticated and layered achievements. And so the more that the self-inflicted accusation gets repeated, the more it sounds like a bad joke becoming increasingly stale. I would not put such a cunning move beyond Ali's capacity for play and his ability to claim and reclaim, using different approaches and producing unexpected outcomes. It would be a risky approach, if this were indeed the approach.

3.

Regarding the Saadi Youssef poem "Vision" that gained some attention during the war on Iraq, the obvious point is that a poet can say whatever he wants and his poems can be taken out of context. Still, the specifics of this situation in a neocolonial world are instructive and disturbing. We have a strange case of consensus among a diverse group of literary professionals who all agreed to highlight the same aspect of a foreign poet's complex vision of his nation. Setting aside the *Los Angeles Times*, whose editorial board supported the war, what did the poem do for those on the left who were against the war? How did they read the poem, and what did they get from it that would distinguish them from those who supported the war? Could it be pessimism—that is, a reflection of the community's resignation, in which the poem served as an unconscious rationalization of their powerlessness? In this case, Youssef's momentary fatalism seems to have affirmed to those opposed to the war that Iraq was indeed a lost cause, exculpating them from having to stop their own governments from starting a neocolonial war. The poet-stranger has a long way to go if the people who supposedly support him use his words against him in this complicated manner.

Metropolitan decontextualization can transpire by subtle means.

Here, a small omission from "A Vision" became an act of tampering. For Youssef and poets like Adrienne Rich and Yannis Ritsos, who are committed to bearing witness, the date of the poem's composition is an important signifier. Youssef marks "Vision" as having been completed on August 13, 1997. This date was not included in any reprinting prior to the war. The date was re-inserted, however, in later postings on the internet by right-wing bloggers; they found in the poem a Nostradamic vision of Iraq that was useful to them during the post-invasion sectarian violence, as Sunnis and Shiites massacred each other.

We can note, in reference to the reprinting of the poem, the wide variety of ways in which the native informant's words can be utilized. In my introduction I praised Saadi Youssef's poetry, showing the voice of the poet as a rich, compact, mobile, and humanizing calling card from one culture to another. Now we see that poetry's discursive technologies can prefigure, in whatever minor way, the indoctrination of the citizenry as a superpower gears up for war. This happens without malice or obvious intent. The poem only appears to tell us that the heart of darkness has moved to another location; it is now in Iraq, and the metropolis has native testimony from that location to prove it.

Now let me turn to the poetry reading with the Iraqi poet Dunya Mikhail and the American poet Brian Turner, where the audience did not have any questions for Mikhail. We note the geographical reversals taking place in the two poets' work: an Iraqi woman who has experienced war in her country is no longer keen on sharing only the poetry about that part of her experience. She has lived in exile for several years now and considers that to be her most pressing subject. Turner, the white male soldier poet, comes to share his experiences about a war he opposed, where at each encounter "with an Iraqi I had a flag and a gun separating me from them." She is writing away from Iraq, and he is digging deeper into that subject matter. Doubtlessly, the neocolonial moment is complicated by the poet-stranger's gender. Does Mikhail's refusal to be a victim render her invisible, her voice undesirable? Is she asking for equality when she speaks her experiences and is being dismissed for doing so? Is the audience ashamed of the damage they caused her country and simply can't bear asking her any questions?

This notion of poetry as exploration of the heart of darkness, which entered into the public reading of Saadi Youssef's "Visions," coupled with the illuminating vision of the reluctant soldier, was on display at the poetry and violence panel. The audience may not have been certain of Mikhail's story—perhaps the Iraq-Iran war seemed to them merely ordinary business for people from that part of the world. What did make a difference were the presence and the bearing of witness by the representative of the neocolonial power, a bona fide citizen like the members of the audience who not only went into the heart of darkness but also now suffers the guilt of having gone there. That Mikhail wanted to transcend the violence she had witnessed and wished to examine her new life and its exilic complications may have made her less relevant. Turner, on the other hand, was working on a second book about his service in Iraq, and clearly there is an audience for his testimony. Who needs a foreign poet when a metropolitan poet is available to tell the war story?[5]

If this sounds like one of the arguments used to disparage Tagore nine decades ago, then the reader has guessed correctly. Here's what one of Tagore's English reviewers wrote about his work: "Those who wish to be impressed by glimpses of a life that is different from our own, by revelation of the Eastern mind which works in a way we can never understand, would do far better to go to Mr. Kipling for what they want" (quoted in Sen 16). The reviewer's comment is relevant and is a blunt, hostile version of what can take place now. First of all, Tagore's reviewer appears to contradict himself; he seems to be saying, "If you wish to understand the Eastern mind, go to Kipling." But he is not saying that; he is saying, "If you wish to be *impressed by . . . revelation* of the Eastern mind." In this nowfamiliar Orientalist discourse, the other can only be experienced as an "impression" and through "revelation," something that needs to be uncovered and experienced in intermittent, peripatetic glimpses. This is all that Kipling–who is the best available source for such experience and much better at it than Tagore–can offer, because the Eastern mind cannot be understood. Interacting with that mind requires the use of different verbs. The native testimony, therefore, represents raw evidence; it is a slippery, barely visible object, and the metropolitan's examination of it is the act of agency. What's the use of a native informant who does not wish to provide the story that the metropolitan audience wants to hear?

What is *the story* here then, and why does the metropolitan audience want to know it? The war with Iraq is taking place *there*, and, like Vietnam before it, the danger Iraq presents is mostly hypothetical. The reason for the war, as most of the American populace convinced itself, was to avenge 9/11, rather than any elaborate threat such as the communist menace. What the metropolitan who is resigned to his nation's warring ways wants to know is how this war out there will affect him. Clearly, there has to be an emotional blowback, and the metropolitan has learned to anticipate it.

In his recent book *Postcolonial Melancholia*, Paul Gilroy addresses the ennui that white Britons have been feeling regarding the profound change in their circumstances that followed the end of empire and the loss of imperial prestige. He attributes this ongoing melancholia to British failure to work through complex feelings of loss and culpability, writing that the British prefer instead to depreciate, discredit, and forget the disquieting, violent history that produced the melancholia in the first place. The American approach, as represented in similar conversations with exiled and diasporic intellectuals and as led by independent metropolitan academics and intellectuals, is perhaps a preemptive effort to address this oncoming neocolonial melancholy. This approach complements the several adjustments that the United States has made since Vietnam. Along with the reduction in the number of American casualties came the reduction of the public's visual exposure to the war (no flag-draped coffins on television or in the newspapers), the reduction of the visual appearance of the civilian victims of warfare, and, finally, the reduction of the soldiers' experience of the living bodies that they would end up killing through the use of robots, drones, and other advanced forms of technology. Real warfare became similar to the guilt-free electronic simulation of war. The final step in this process was to anticipate the anxiety among the public about violence taking place in their name and about the return of soldiers suffering from post-traumatic stress disorders, bearing physical and emotional scars as reminders of a greater violence. Poetry is important here as it reflects where metropolitan anxieties lie. One of the questions most commonly addressed to Turner was whether his poems had helped *him* maintain his psyche and his emotional balance (see Turner, 2007, 2008, and "Rewrite").

4.

If the divisions in this discussion—metropolitan and postcolonial, subject and object, native informant and neocolonial agent, ethnic and exile—seem too divisive, standing as unbridgeable binaries, it is because there was much at stake in the cases I am referring to, and such contingent moments harden the membranes of the societal body in which the diasporic, exilic, or foreign poet operates. Unrelated to the Iraq conflict, the Shahid Ali story I related took place a few months after 9/11, as U.S. troops had begun their campaign in Afghanistan, not far from the poet's birthplace. And though I do not see a direct connection between the relaying of Shahid Ali's "darkie" story and the 9/11 events, the telling of that story occurred in that atmosphere. Additionally, though taking complex individual stances, Turner and Mikhail do stand as metonyms of the two nations involved in the war, at least within the panel I'm referring to. Amalgamated, hybrid identities such as Mikhail's are challenged by such crises, and so the poet-stranger speaks, aware of the continuum between the binaries in which she stands and the flexible positions she may need to occupy to speak her piece.

It's worth our effort now to contextualize these and similar conversations and exchanges. Cultural exchanges among modern nation-states have served various functions, from creating diplomatic openings to cementing relations after trade and military agreements have been ratified. Countries at war, on the other hand, do not invite each other's poets into their midst. Such power is the prerogative of the metropolis, and the stories I have relayed are incidents about the dynamics of uneven exchange. A metropolis can do many things at the same time—it can capture those who declare war against its plans, it can bomb their civilians, it can build schools and hospitals there, and it can write a country's constitution for it. It can also vaccinate the children, remove land mines, and fertilize the farmland as it continues the killing.

Needless to say, knowledge contributes to all these advantages, and individuals—poets included—are involved in these circuits of knowledge/power exchange. If speaking to the metropolis is not teachable per se, it can be learned, and a postcolonial individual can easily acquire the working paradigms and the most efficient stylistic approaches and mannerisms toward that end. Penetrable as it may be, however, the metropolis can—and often does—decide whom the spokesperson for the other is going to be. Facing such power, it is not surprising that many poet-strangers who establish reputations in the metropolis stand in awkward positions. The example of the late Palestinian poet Taha Muhammad Ali serves as an interesting case in how these dynamics play out. Taha Ali was a schoolteacher who also had made a living as a seller "of Christian trinkets to Jewish tourists" (*New York Times*) in his Nazareth shop. His poetry occupies only three pages in Salma Jayyusi's authoritative *Anthology of Modern Palestinian Literature*. A long list of other poets are given more space, with Darwish occupying a lion's share. Though not considered a major poet at home, Taha Ali has become one of the best-known international poets in America and Europe since the leading poetry presses in the United States and the United Kingdom published his poetry a few years ago. His volume of selected poems, *So What*, has gone through several printings. Recently, Yale University Press published a major biography of Taha Ali; it is the only biography in English of a modern Arab poet. Ali is virtually unknown in the Arab world, and he is known in Palestine more as a short story writer than a poet.

It will not surprise the reader that Taha Ali's poetry is not confrontational or that "he has rarely written declamatory political poetry" (*New York Times*). Taha Ali's political views regarding the Palestinian-Israeli conflict are subtly expressed and may even be considered pacifistic. His biographer and translator, respectively, are an American Jewish couple who live in West Jerusalem, the Israeli side of the city. Is this a case where the metropolis has found someone who knows to speak to it, or, inversely, has it found someone whose voice it deems "authentic"?

There are many aspects of Taha Ali that make him appeal as a natural, as opposed to a national, poet. In performance, he relies on his translator to read the English versions of his poetry, but he often tells in his halting English long and amusing stories about people from his village, which the Israelis had razed in 1948. Taha Ali gives a compelling performance and often enough receives standing ovations among U.S. audiences. Interestingly, there has been a strange silence among Palestinian intellectuals in the United States regarding what has come to be known as "The Taha Effect." Among the Palestinian writers I have spoken to, Taha Ali's success is seen as at least harmless to their cause, and certainly no one wants to begrudge the man his success. But he is no Darwish, and he is not considered a true spokesperson in terms of the esthetic ambitions of his work or of the ongoing confrontation with neocolonial Israel. "Why him?" is a question I have often heard. Is it simply a case of the metropolitan researcher coming to the region and choosing the poet he wishes to export to his home country? Could the situation be as simple as that? Could it be simpler still in that it is merely a case of a poet-translator and a biographer finding a poet whose work they admire and can translate and present admirably to the metropolitan world? Is such simplicity still possible when the terms of the cultural exchange are so uneven between the two settings?

5.

This brings us to the issue of translation in its most specific and widest sense. Taha Ali's poetry, full of imagery and direct exposition, is easy to translate. His language lacks innuendo and double entendres, and since it is written in free verse, the translator need not have a guilty conscience about losing the specific musicality of the original. Darwish's poetry, on the other hand, presents a greater challenge; it is extremely difficult to bring forth all the textual and aural allusions he makes in his poetry. For example, in the poem "Al-Qurban" ("Blood Offering"), Darwish uses the rhyming end-words from Surat Maryam, the Mary, mother of Jesus, chapter in the Quran, which tells the story of the immaculate conception and birth of Christ. The use of these rhyming end-words provides a Quranic musical allusion that most of his Arabic readers and listeners easily recognize. Juxtaposing the martyr with Christ's crucifixion, Darwish blends Islamic scripture with Christian theology, a complex and daring maneuver that rests on the use of these rhyming end words. One need not worry about similarly complicated matters in Taha Ali's work. His poems do have their own power, but it is a power that does not defy translation.

As to what to choose among a poet's work and what gets to be translated, the process is irregular to say the least. I have been asked several times how I chose my selections of a poet's work and why I had chosen a given poet in the first place, and I never felt that I gave a satisfactory answer. I usually answer that my choices depended on my taste and on what I came up with in the translation. I also say that I always seek the poet's approval of my selections of her or his work. In the case of Saadi Youssef, who is one of the most important poets that I have translated so far, I specifically consulted with two well-known Arabic poetry specialists, and both found my choices representative of the poet's work.

But that is no consolation either, as it could be argued that the poet, the scholars, and myself have, like Tagore once did, a notion of what "the West" wants—and that could also be misguided. One obvious advantage that the scholars, the poet, and I may have regarding the metropolitan audience is that we are members of it, capable of seeing it from within its poetic traditions and esthetic inclinations. I should also point out that metropolitan audiences are *not* monolithic, as they were not in Tagore's time; interest in Tagore's work and persona lasted longer in the rest of Europe than it did in England and America. Further more, metropolitan audiences and readerships tend to prefer their own resident poet-strangers. Mahmoud Darwish, who once lived in France, and the Syrian poet Adonis, who lives there now, have literary agents in Paris, and their works are more widely available in French than they are in English. Similarly, Joseph Brodsky and Czesław Milosz—who came to the United States during the Cold War and lived in the United States and wrote in their native languages—were more readily available in English during that period than they were even in their native languages. In the Soviet Bloc, Nazim Hikmet, the most important Turkish poet of the twentieth century, became well known shortly after World War II; his first translation into English appeared in the United States in the 1980s. This is to say that exiled writers can become localized; they can become more important in the metropolis than they are in their native countries and languages. Their authenticity as representatives of their nations, regions, or languages depends on their presence in the metropolis and their statuses as exiles, rather than being resident natives.

Furthermore, the agents involved in the process of translation respond and act according to the contingencies in which the cultural exchange takes place. The poet Willis Barnstone, my friend and former teacher, tells the story of how his translation of Mao Zedong's poetry languished at a major publishing house in New York for nine months before they called him asking if he would translate Chairman Mao. The book came out eight days after he reminded them that they already had the manuscript. This, of course, happened in 1973, on the heels of the famous episode of Ping-Pong diplomacy. Mao, the poet, was not the first author of communist lineage to benefit from translation in this manner. Certainly, Brodsky's emergence and subsequent career were affected positively by Cold War politics. For writers from Muslim countries in the post-Cold War world, the words "fatwa" and "translation" have become a natural pairing. When Muslim fundamentalists in Bangladesh issued a fatwa against the Bangladeshi poet Taslima Nasrin, her profile rose dramatically in a manner reminiscent of the Rushdie affair. In Egypt, for example, and elsewhere in the Arab world, there is such cynicism regarding any erotic or religiously offensive work that authors are often accused of being opportunists seeking to have a fatwa issued against them so that they will be translated into Western languages. The case of Salwa Al-Neimi's recent novel *Burhān al-'Asal* (*Honey's Irrefutable Proof*, 2007) is a case in point (see Jross 2006 and Man'a 2008). Not long after the publication of her book, she was accused of writing for the purpose of translation—in other words, of writing a book that would be banned by Arabic censors and that would immediately be picked up by Western publishers, which is where the real money comes from. In the meantime, Nasrin continues to write and to struggle with religious censorship in India, where she lives in exile. But interest in her work has decreased since the initial fatwa-driven excitement. The point I'm trying to make here is that such interest is not merely marketing gimmickry, but that such gimmickry does exploit a significant component of the nature of the dynamics of cultural exchange between the metropolis and the peripheries.

6.

Increasingly, translation is playing a more important role in the diasporic poet's writing process and in the lives and experiences of diasporic communities. The question here is: Who needs translation to assist his or her position in the metropolis and how can translation enable them? The Arab communities in the United States who invited Mudhafar al-Nawab either did not think they needed to share their cultural heritage, or thought that he was *not* what they wish to have translated. In other words, in the same way that the metropolis decides to highlight certain figures from given cultures, diasporic representatives of these cultures also have a say, even if in a negative manner, in what gets translated. Al-Nawab is a fiery poet whose views are critical of Arab regimes and U.S. policies in the region. His poetry, reminiscent of Darwish's early work, utilizes simple language but has strong musical registers, and it includes many allusions to current and ancient Arab history, elements that make his poetry difficult to translate. His importance to his Arabic audience here in the United States is in remaining beyond translation.

On the other hand, Arab-American literary activists have developed strong links with translation. The late Edward Said was actively involved in promoting the translation of Arabic novels into English. Said often recalled an experience with his publisher, who had asked him to prepare a list of Third World authors whose works might be translated. The publisher accepted many of the writers he recommended, Said said. But when Said asked why Egyptian writer Nagib Mahfouz was excluded, he was told that Mahfouz's "works are in Arabic and Arabic is a controversial language" (Gabriel 2002). Lending his name and prestige to various translation projects over the last three decades, Said wrote several prefaces and blurbs for works of Arab literature in translation. Also, the recent vigor around translating Darwish has been led by Arab-American poets and translators. The few books of Adonis's poetry in translation have all been the work of Arab-American scholars.

There is clearly a functional aspect to all of this. The diasporic Arab community, which is beset by misrepresentation of its cultural heritage and labeled as made up of religious fanatics and terrorists, is keen on showing the modernized and secular facets of its society, among which contemporary literature stands as a major achievement. This interest in the arts coincides with Darwish's initiative in Palestine to promote esthetics as a means of generating international identification with the Palestinians.

7.

As to what the poet-stranger gets in return for his investment in his native literature and its promotion in a metropolitan setting, the case of Shahid Ali proves quite instructive again. For one thing, Ali's (poet-stranger's) esthetic project and his poet persona rest on an investment in his native literature and its promotion in his metropolitan setting. Along with his promotion of the ghazal, Shahid Ali also translated and edited *The Rebel's Silhouette* (1991), a volume of selected poems by Faiz Ahmed Faiz (1911–84), the most celebrated modern poet of the Urdu language. It should be noted also that, in the late 1970s and early 1980s, Shahid Ali was perhaps the only poet of an Urdu-language background writing in the United States. With his verse drawing on his eclectic knowledge of Anglo-American prosody, Shahid Ali was virtually on his own, his poetry not part of any discernable tradition.

This element of the poet-stranger's pronounced estrangement from the canon to which he is contributing is typical of the poets of our century. In *Beginnings*, Edward Said notes that writers in the West, beginning in the late nineteenth century, have had to become autodidacts, each "gathering or making up the knowledge one needs in the course of creating." (*Beginnings* 8) This had become the case "because the past [began to] appear less useful" (8) to the modern writer. This same past would also invariably seem useless for the poet-stranger, who is trying to enter the metropolitan literary culture in its present incarnation. Like poet-strangers, metropolitan writers also cannot find a place for themselves in their literature or in any cultural "continuity that formerly stretched forward and backward in time" (9). The poet-stranger may not have a choice to accept or refuse such continuity, as he may find it impossible to feel part of a past alien to him and where he cannot see himself reflected.

Nonetheless, the poet-stranger, also like writers of his generation in the metropolis, still needs texts in which his own work would fit "by adjacency, not sequentially or dynastically" (10). This is where the exiled/diasporic writer's native tradition can come to his aid. Transported to his new surroundings, his tradition will not bear on him with its weight of precedence and will not fill him with a sense of belatedness. In this regard, translation can enable the diasporic poet, allowing him to compose texts that can be read alongside his own. Translating one's native literary inheritance saves the poet-stranger "from his contemporaries," as Kenneth Rexroth once noted (Rexroth 1959), making the point that a poet must try to avoid sounding like them, feeling compelled to address the same subject matter, or engaging in their formal projects. Translation offers the poet-stranger a wider esthetic and idiomatic plain than his contemporaries in the metropolis have.

Furthermore, translation can regift the diasporic poet his language and help him create a language inflected with that of his national origin. Similar to Walcott's adoption, in "The Schooner Flight," of the voice of Shabine, a character who imbued Walcott's verse with a regional vigor, the flavor of translation in Shahid Ali's case allowed him to claim a variety of English that only he could write in believably. Looking at two passages from Shahid Ali's poetry, we can see that he moved toward an English flavored with translation (and perhaps with his translations of Faiz). Here are a few lines from the poem "Postcard from Kashmir," which appeared in *The Half-Inch Himalayas* (1987):

> *Kashmir shrinks into my mailbox,*
> *my home a neat four by six inches.*
> *I always loved neatness. Now I hold*
> *the half-inch Himalayas in my hand.*

And here are lines from the aforementioned "Ghazal I," first published in 1997:

> *Don't weep, we'll drown out the Calls to Prayer, O Saqi—*
> *I'll raise my glass before wine is defiled by exiles.*
>
> *Was—after the last sky—this the fashion of fire:*
> *Autumn's mist pressed to ashes styled by exiles?*

The difference in the two passages is discernable in the syntax, tone, and diction. The first passage is sentence-driven, composed of a basic structure of subject-verb-object. Its dialogue is a hushed one between poet and reader. In the second passage, the sentences are divided among a congregation of subjects. First, the Saqi (wine server) is addressed in second person, then the utterance becomes a statement in first-person plural, and then it returns to first-person singular. The second sentence in the second passage is a question with two major interruptions. The utterances in both couplets of the ghazal are dramatic and full of gestures; and the language, with its archaic O and commanding authority, sounds as if it is being shouted from a stage.

Most importantly, while the first passage addresses the experience of exile, the second sends the poet home and places him, despite translation, deeply inside his tradition and its poetics. Furthermore, the language of the second passage is reminiscent of Edward FitzGerald's translation of Omar al-Khayyam's *Rubaiyat*. Shahid Ali mimics this linguistic register and makes it his own. Not only is Shahid Ali, the diasporic poet, translating his heritage, he is claiming outright the colonizer's reproductions of his tradition's gifts. And it is perhaps within this sort of complex maneuvering that we can place Ali's use of the term "darkie," an expression so exuberantly displaced that it borders on celebration.

8.

A Libyan proverb I grew up hearing says, "Become a stranger and start telling lies." In a land of vast distances, the further away one moved from one's origins, the more she or he is able to invent herself or himself to be able to survive. It's arguable that half of America is made up of such renamed people, and that that renaming took place even before Ellis Island imposed new names on the newcomers. People renamed themselves even without being forced to do so, made up life stories, and told the lies that better suited their aspirations.

Similarly, though with a harrowing subtext, the poet and Holocaust survivor Paul Celan once said, "Only in one's mother tongue can one express one's own truth. In a foreign language the poet lies" (quoted in Kligerman 108). Celan was raised speaking Romanian and Yiddish as well as German. Like Kafka, he was a member of what Deleuze and Guattari call a deterritorialized community. Since Celan also wrote some poems in Romanian, it is hard to be certain as to which language was foreign to him. Celan spoke French and knew it very well. His comment about the poet lying came as an answer to a question regarding his relationship to French and why he did not write in it. Though Celan considered French a foreign language to him, it may have aided his German and inflected his voice when writing in it, in the same way that Shahid Ali's Urdu had a palimpsestic echo under his English. Surely, Celan's Romanian also added another linguistic register to his poetry.

The point is that Celan's choice of German was not inevitable and may have been strategic, not in practical but, in psychological terms. "In employing the language of his mother [German], Celan chooses to enter in conversation with those responsible for the death of his parents and the destruction of his home," argues Kligerman (108). Celan's choice of language is perhaps the opposite of a mask, a metapoetic device meant to mop up any traces of irony or detachment that the German reader may develop while hearing or reading him. A living indictment even when not speaking in those terms, Celan's poetry thus bears elements of performance—in this case, the heartbreaking performance of grief and mourning.

This brings me to the adjustment I'd like to make here to Celan's declaration, in which I find much truth. I would like to adjust his hunch by restating his dictum in this way: "In a foreign setting, the poet-stranger performs his truth." This helps me understand Shahid Ali and many others coming from elsewhere and presenting themselves as strangers to strangers. As long ago as 1709, three Iroquois kings arrived in London and, when asked to address an audience of dignitaries, decided to dress up in clothes they chose from the Queen Theatre's wardrobe. They were there on display and decided to embellish their image, perhaps to heighten their authenticity using non-authentic implements, and with an instinctive understanding that all authenticities are to some degree "planned" (Trinh 98).

A version of that understanding also operates in the self-presentation of the modern world's most illustrious poet-strangers: in Tagore's self-presentation as an Eastern sage in the early twentieth century; in Walcott's search for the appropriate poetic mask; and in Darwish's persona of "lover of the Palestine," when he was bringing his community together in the early 1960s and declaiming their belonging to the land of their birth, and later still as a chronicler of the Palestinians' anguish-filled saga. The poet-stranger understands he is on show, both subject and object of projection, and that while he makes his best effort to embody a universal humanity, his very gestures toward that end could well be seen as signs of his irreparable strangeness. Let's just say that some poets are adept at swimming against the tide of misinterpretation. Some are icebreakers who chug through opposing ice. The question for readers in the cosmopolitan world is: What do we/they want from the the poet-strangers that they/we invite among their/our midst? Yes, it is a big world open to all, and the great cities of the world have become much more hospitable. But there are wars, too; new ones and more devastating ones that democracies initiate and sustain. And there are populations displaced, cities demolished, and much guilt to preempt and erase. What conditions will we create for the strangers among us to speak? What do we want to hear from them?

Notes

1. Perhaps one of the best expressions of this testy insider's stance is the model provided by South African poet Breyten Breytenbach. Breytenbach sees the function of the postcolonial poet in the metropolis as being a contentious provider of awareness ("Exile" 180). The exile, or "intruder," Breytenbach explains, is at the mercy of the "the host" ("Letter"15) but must also assume a challenging pose. As the postcolonial learns "the chameleon art of adaptation," he must "never again entirely relax the belly muscles" ("Exile" 180). The exile must carry an aura of invincibility and even superiority. "You demand to be treated respectfully, your edges become sharper and your paranoia more acute. . . . You are invited to New York for a conference? Insist upon being put up in the best hotel?" (180). For the postcolonial in the metropolis to be an effective advocate, he "must husband [his] weaknesses" (180). "You make sure that you are tougher than 'they' are, or you damn well learn how to pretend to be" (180). Breytenbach advances this masculine exilic approach as the best way to serve the masses of Africa and the downtrodden elsewhere. If the postcolonial intruder "starts want-

ing to be treated on an equal footing," his hosts will "tear him to pieces" (Breytenbach, "Letter" 15). Not allowed equality in the metropolis as he pleads his noble causes, the postcolonial intellectual claims superiority, threatening his hosts with a world that can "vomit at unexpected moments" ("Exile" 180).

2. Describing his friend Joseph Brodsky, Walcott outlines his role within the metropolis. He sees in Brodsky the ideal model of an exile who is "an irascible guest" (*Twilight* 142). Walcott tells us that Brodsky "does not flatter the torturer or the system . . . nor has he rushed into the lowered arms of the Statue of Liberty, afraid of being burnt by her torch" (142). Noting that Brodsky is a Soviet exile in the United States, Walcott adds that the Russian poet "has written under two self-idealizing democracies, America and the Soviet Russia" (142), and swiftly equates the two superpowers, a gesture of his own irascibility. Brodsky is an exile who refuses to help "ensure the perpetuity of the republic. He does not glorify his hosts. . . . He seems to be inhabiting his own country, muttering a complicated monologue which does not simplify its references, and whose spirit not to lament but to cherish disinheritance" (142).

3. Here's the full passage by James Joyce referred to here: "And I will try to express myself in some mode of life or art as freely as I can and as wholly as I can, using for my defence the only arms I allow myself to use, silence, exile and cunning."

4. In a similar gesture and approach, Walcott, as his biographer reports, had on occasion to calm Robert Lowell's nerves, letting him know that he was not in the United States to compete with him, that they were working on different subject matters (King 377).

5. The Vietnam war literature is a case in point. How many literary accounts do we have available that tell the Vietnam story from the Vietnamese point of view on the shelves of the metropolitan libraries? And if the victor is the one that gets to tell the story, who, then, won the war?

Works Cited

Ali, Agha Shahid. *A Nostalgist's Map of America.* New York: Norton: 1991.
Ali, Agha Shahid. *Call Me Ishmail, Tonight: A Book of Ghazals.* New York: Norton: 2003.
Ali, Agha Shahid. *Half-Inch Himalayas.* Middletown, CT: Wesleyan UP, 1987.
Ali, Agha Shahid. *Rooms Are Never Finished.* New York: Norton: 2001.
Ali, Agha Shahid. *The Country without a Post Office.* New York: Norton: 1997.
Ali, Agha Shahid and Sara Suleri. "The Ghazal" *Ravishing DisUnities.* Middletown, CT: Wesleyan University, 2000.
Breytenbach, Breyten. "The Exile as African." In *Together Elsewhere: Writers on Exile,* Marc Robinson, editor. Winchester, MA: Faber and Faber, 1994.

Breytenbach, Breyten. "A Letter from Exile, to Don Espejuelo; In *Together Elsewhere: Writers on Exile*, Marc Robinson, editor. Winchester, MA: Faber and Faber, 1994.

Garner, Dwight. "A Merchant of Trinkets and Memories" *New York Times*, May 5, 2009. http://www.nytimes.com/2009/05/06/books/06garn.html

Joyce, James. *A Portrait of the Artist as a Young Man*. London: B.W. Huebsch, 1916.

Kligerman, Eric. *Sites of the Uncanny: Paul Celan, Specularity and the Visual Arts*. New York: Walter de Gruyter, 2007.

Naimi, Salwa. *Burhan Al-'Asal*. [*Hoeny's Irrefutable Proof*] Damascus: Cadmus lil-Nashr, 2007.

Rexroth, Kenneth. "The Poet as Translator." 1959. http://www.bopsecrets.org/rexroth/essays/poetry-translation.htm

Robinson, Marc, ed. *Elsewhere: Writers on Exile*. Winchester, MA: Faber and Faber, 1994.

Said, Edward. *Beginnings: Intention and Method*. New York: Columbia University, 1985.

Sen, Nabaneeta. "An Aspect of Tagore-Criticism in the West: The Cloud of Mysticism." *Mahfil: A Quarterly of South Asian Literature* 3.1 (1996): 9–23.

Trinh, T. Minh-Ha. *Women, Native, Other: Writing Postcoloniality and Feminism*. Bloomington: Indiana University Press, 1989.

Turner, Brian. "A Conversation with Brian Turner" interview with Patrick Hicks. *Virginia Quarterly Review Online*, 2008.

Turner, Brian. "Interview with Brian Turner" Elaine Riot, *Rewrite*.

Turner, Brian. "War and Peace: An Interview with Poet Brian Turner" with Stefene Russell. *St. Louis Magazine* (April 2009).

Youssef, Saadi. *Without an Alphabet, Without a Face*. Translated by Khaled Mattawa. St. Paul, MN: Graywolf Press, 2002.

Identity, Power and a Prayer for Repatriation
On Translating and Writing Poetry

I.

In December 1988, in my last year in college, I travelled for a week to New York and took Lorca's *Poet in New York* with me. I realize the narcissism implied in the sentence, but I'd been carrying the book with me for months at the time. And while on Atlantic Avenue in Brooklyn a day or so later, in an Arab grocery story, I found some books of Mahmoud Darwish. Back in the room where I was staying, I'd read a poem by Lorca and put it aside, read some Darwish and translated it into English, and then went back to Lorca, and so on. In between, I wrote some of my own lines. I didn't know Spanish, but I could read Lorca out loud for cadence. And there was Darwish's Arabic, and my own versions of his poetry in English. I had four floods of poetry coming at me, and what I put down was perhaps an expression of the whirlpool they created in me.

Being inspired to write while reading happens to all poets and happens to composers as well. They start playing something by another composer and then their own "original" work comes through. Other than directly quoting Arab poets in my work, I've yet to understand how translation contributes to my process of composition, except to say that, like rhyme or meter or any rule we set up for our poems, translation adds a focus on precision, the focus that forces one to be creative.

This episode in Brooklyn happened nine years into my life in the United States, where I came at the age of fourteen—fully aware of who I am in a cultural sense. I was a foreigner and knew that alterity would stay with me for some time. I felt that foreignness when I first read Walt Whitman. His America just did not speak to me then. I needed something in English but that was also in my "language." Translating Arab poets offered me a chance to experiment with sensibilities similar to mine (using familiar images, symbols, and motifs) in English. Contemporary poets wrote poems based on exercises, others wrote imitations as beginners. Earlier poets, Milton included, cut their chops on translations from Latin and Hebrew. I chose this more old-fashioned apprenticeship, except that I did not do this for the exercise but for the kinship.

Translating Darwish was also a sentimental education. As a political refugee, I was uncertain about where I'd end up or where I wanted to be, and I was aware that I'd been gone too long, that the link between my upbringing and my early adulthood had many gaps, which were the only place I could exist. Americans are now more aware of the difficulties faced by immigrants from my region, but back in the 1980s, Arab-bashing was gratuitous. That went along with the Reagan administration's policies of global racism (support of South Africa's apartheid, numerous wars in Africa, persecution of Palestinians, and funding the murderous regimes of Central America). Who would stay in a country like that if he had a choice? In the old days, one would call this state alienation, political, social, and cultural. In an early, romantic view of poetry, such alienation can take the poet a long way.

Privileged with or disadvantaged by alienation as the case may be, what I found interesting about Lorca's *Poet in New York* was his delirious anger against the modernity machine. An Andalusian, he was so enraptured and frightened by New York that he turned the city into a theater, where an ancient nightmarish vision of Dante's *Inferno* met surrealism, where folk mythology fused with a modern underworld creeping up the skyscrapers. In *Poet in New York*, Lorca confronts what García-Márquez called "a reality that is in itself out of all proportion" (Mendoza 60). In that case, realism, or the lyric voice grounded in shared knowledge, was not appropriate. Lorca needed an athletic imagination to protect himself from being dissolved and sent streaming down the many drains that populate the poems in that book.

A sense of political grievance, anger at feeling trapped (albeit in America), along with a desire to preserve something which was about to be lost, were what I had brought with me to write poetry. I was writing in English and my sensibility was rooted in a vision that needed to be translated. Not surprisingly, I found great affinity in poets like Pablo Neruda, Cesar Vallejo, Constantine Cavafy, and, most of all, Nazim Hikmet, who happened to be poets of exile. This sense of alterity helped me connect with certain American poets, too. Philip Levine's poetry had a generous justifiable anger that I could embrace. How was that clarity of purpose we find in Levine's work derived from his reading of Spanish poets, the ones he translated and others he read in translation, I don't quite know. Let's just say, as far as I was concerned, every American poet I latched into, had about him or her the scent of translation. Translation was the sweat and frankincense of home, variable and the same.

Translation is something I encounter on a daily basis. As soon as I say my name, I've put myself outside the border; I have to crawl back into the center. When a stranger asks me my name—and they ask maybe four or five times a day—every time they ask they're telling me "I don't know this name." Then I have to find a way to translate or legitimate the existence of my name in this world, in their language. Translation, not alienation or estrangement, becomes a kind of existential state, a form of identity.

At home in Libya after years of living away, and in the enigmatic state of arrival, I spent my first day in the banal world of funeral wakes, where customary words such as '*Azzana wahid* are exchanged among the attendees. '*Azzana wahid.* The phrase is repeated a thousand times, its meaning buried in the automatic perception of ritualized utterance where heartfelt sentiment dies. '*Azzana wahid* means "our grief is one." Our . . . grief . . . is . . . one . . . During the noisy nonchalant gatherings of my father's funeral in Libya, only in translation, in my English, did the words "our grief is one" mean anything to me. I culled that solace from mouths that did not mean to touch me so deeply, and it was translation that allowed me to enter like an endoscope lens into the mourners' hearts to retrieve the comfort I needed. Proof again that identities are made, or scooped, or dug, never quite passed on, or given. That effort in reading the words beyond the words people said, the quiet probing of what my countrymen were trying to really tell me and my need to translate them, was how I began to seek my return, my place at home.

II.

Back in 1986, a few months after Reagan's bombing of Libya, my parents and I, in Greece at the time, went to the American embassy to apply for a visa for them to come visit my brother and me. I had arranged for the appointment a few weeks earlier, and we showed up an hour early. When the interview time came, I walked up with my father to the bureaucrat behind the bulletproof glass. Recognizing somehow that my father spoke no English, she asked if we have a translator. I said, "I'll translate for him." Then after shuffling through the application forms for some time, she asked my father, "Why do you want to come to America?" My father said "*Siyaha*," (the Arabic word for "tourism"). I, translating him said, "He wants to visit my brother and me, and spend some time with us, see the country a little bit . . ." The consular official interrupted me and said "OK, stop! He said one word, and you're going on and on. That's why we don't like family members translating for applicants. This interview is over." She collected the papers and went back inside.

Let me clarify that we were not destitute, but members of a comfortable middle class, and, indeed, if my parents were to come and visit, it really was to see my brother and me. In those days, any Libyan living in the United States and not registered with Qaddafi's People's Bureau, was suspect. Several returnees from the United States we knew were arrested upon arrival and spent years in prison, and as usual, without charges. Not refugees, and not starving, my brother and I were still not protected from the capriciousness of Qaddafi's regime.

My reaction to the consular official's quick dismissal of us was to stand dumbfounded, if not ashamed. Having been a kind of exile for some years, I thought I was adept at "translating" my background and myself. My encounter at the American embassy was the first attempt to translate the United States, if you will, to my background, to my family. And when my father asked me what would come out of our brief interview, I lied, and for the life of me, I can't remember the lie I told him.

There's subservience in this kind of translation, and maybe in all translation, in the attempt to smooth out kinks of difference, and to make the powerful less powerful, and the powerless less powerless. That's how I interpret my effusiveness in translating my father's one-word answer. I thought he needed help, and that the American consular official needed help understanding us. I had forgotten then that my father's cryptic answer was how he had operated for decades before authorities of all kinds. I am certain that when he faced the Libyan Internal Security officer at the Benghazi airport, his answer was also the passive-aggressive phrase of "tourism," and in a tone that was neither defiant nor solicitous, lugubriously nonchalant, with no admission of need, and confident that that moment will pass. People in authority distrust being loved and may love being feared, but are generally impotent before apathy. They can't stand people who refuse to be translated.

Somewhere in my work as a translator, this thought still offers considerable guidance. Translation does occur between parties of equal power—between Norwegians and Italians, for example. But much of what I do as translation does not take place in a cultural détente. This is the legacy of centuries of European dominance in the world, the legacy of the last six decades of American imperialism, Orientalism, the Crusades, and fear of non-whites. As a translator, a person who often faces unbridgeable distances and is forced into finding out how they can be crossed—I, in the American consulate in Athens, wanted to become a kind of ferry, more than willing to bring another to my shore. What I've learned since then is that when we commit acts of generosity out of weakness, we set ourselves up for rejection, and that solicitude is not a viable way to cross distances. What would have happened had I simply said "tourism" while representing my father? I am certain there would have been a follow-up question, more than one.

A literary case in point to explore this idea further: here's how Rabindranath Tagore, the great Indian poet, approached translating his own poems. By the time he was awarded the Nobel Prize for literature in 1913, Tagore had helped modernize Bengali and, indeed, all the arts in the Indian subcontinent. His poetry is dense in imagery and conceptual thought and is steeped in the cultural heritage of India. As he rendered his poems to English, he felt "English readers had very little patience for scenes and sentiments that are foreign to them; they feel a sort of grievance for what they do not understand—and they care not to understand whatever is different from their familiar world" (quoted Sengupta 165).

And so Tagore chose poems that English readers would find palatable. In his native Bengali, he had written mostly about secular matters. In English, however, he presented only his devotional poems perhaps because English audiences were familiar with the stereotypical Indian guru persona. He made his poems much more simplistic by "circumvent[ing] areas that offer resistance" (169). Tagore's approach here cannot be reduced to a personal inferiority complex. There was a power imbalance that, acting with a strong sense of agency, he thought could be realigned by appealing to a sense of shared humanity. But as far as his culture was concerned, the British intelligentsia, even before Macaulay's famous minute, had already "read" Tagore. This perceptual stacked deck is what Mahasweta Sangupta calls the "'symbolic order' of the English language where meaning and signification are already fixed according to the differential network of relations" (164). This system "patterns and regulates all thought and action within a given discursive field" (164), leading them to a set of foregone conclusions. A colonized subject like Tagore "seems to have no option but to deploy the symbolic order of the English language which already has an existent repertory of discourse defining the alterity of the East" (164–65).

In other words, the other has already translated you, has fixed you within given parameters. This happens among all different groups, even among Norwegians and Italians where no obvious power struggle ensues. But it's more evident when a power struggle does exist, and within that, there are options for the work to be translated. And that is why readers in the West have grown to expect a kind of one dimensionality in the work of writers from problematic regions most evident in marketing of such works. Here are the familiar types:

1. There's the rebel exile who has resorted to the West for protection and who confirms to them how awful his home country was. He is most useful if his country happens to be an enemy nation.
2. Then there's the aesthete who just wants the freedom to create art and examine the perennial concerns of art, not politics. Invariably, this artist is an elitist and he adds international credibility to the capitalist class structure.
3. Then there's the melancholic exile who bemoans his displacement, and whose work is there to remind Westerners of the charms of the Old World, a lost innocence that Americans particularly find utterly enchanting. His nostalgia confirms their notions of the universal, also their superior advanced cultural status over his native country's.

Deviate from these, show ambivalence, or, God forbid, critique your "hosts" and you're pushed into margins you did not know existed.

Trying to smuggle my voice with Darwish and Lorca serving as my coyotes, I had to think also about how to smuggle myself into a given cultural setting while seeming to surpass or forego any claim or desire for being native and also conscious of being typecast. It seemed enough to be one's own. But encounters with power in the world of writing, even in a field as marginal as poetry, were inevitable. In a symbolic order that had a discriminating taste for which truffles to pick, translation, expressed as the smuggling of foreign goods, and untranslatability—something like the taciturnity of my father's one-word answer—provided a sense of how to resist being consumed, and if swallowed, to be a cause of discomfort.

III.

It is Thursday, July 29th; the Libyan uprising has been going on for five months now and I am in Benghazi, in Idris Ibn Al-Tayyeb's office in the revolutionary government's Ministry of Foreign Affairs. I had come to my home to see my family and to see what I could do on the ground. Beginning with the outbreak of the Libyan revolution, I had made several television appearances, wrote several commentaries, and was constantly online following the news and commenting on developments. Two months into the revolution, my wife and I started working at Libya TV in Qatar to help with the cause.

I had been meeting Idris over the past few days, and we had talked about, among other things, a peace plan that would enable Qaddafi to leave Libya safely after surrendering power to a group of technocrats acceptable to revolutionaries. "How to fuse the body of Qaddafi's state and the new National Transitional Council?" Idris wondered aloud, inviting me to think with him. Driving through Benghazi's cop-less streets, where fellow drivers rode four-by-fours with anti-aircraft guns installed on top and ignored traffic rules with abandon, and where a sense of glee mingled with palpable panic regarding the future of the state, I found much to think about. Terms like "reconciliation," "transitional justice," "constitution," and "decentralization" were being bandied about among the people I had been meeting and the talking heads on the TV channel I worked with in Qatar. But the words were not promising: they were like lumps of sand flung on a dry wall and not sticking, or the proverbial spaghetti noodles flung at a wet wall, quickly slithering down.

In that atmosphere, I sought Idris because he had been a kind of anchor for me in Libya over the past few years. I also came to tell him that I had translated a poem of his, a poem addressed to the city of Tripoli, whose liberation we'd all been anticipating. Idris had written the poem in prison in the late 1970s, where he spent ten years altogether. A symbolist piece typical of the poetry written at the time, Idris's poem imagines the city as a beloved woman caught in the chains of tyranny whom the poet frees, redeeming himself in the process. It was not a poem that had caught my eye prior to the revolution, but given the living longing for the city to unchain itself from the regime, the poem came alive, and I thought it deserved to be translated. But even as I translated the poem, I wondered who would read it, and why publish it on a website whose readers generally do not read poetry in translation. I wondered if I should be translating it into English at all. Nonetheless, I felt I had at least done something for my good friend Idris and to tell him in so many words that his words and mine have at last fused.

On one level, Idris and I have had a kind of friendship that I'd had with several Arab poets, a friendship marked by a tension over my ability to introduce them to a new world of readers. Often enough, they are poets whose poems do not come to any good in my own words or my diction. I should say that my view of Arabic poetry has been affected by my ability to translate it. If I am not challenged to translate a poem, I find it difficult to appreciate and connect with. And so I had been underappreciating Idris's until his poem in Tripoli spoke to me.

But appreciating and admiring Idris himself is what I had done for years. He's a remarkable man. He'd had polio as a child. Due to his handicap, his father sent him to a religious cloister in a distant oasis, where he memorized the Quran and studied to be an imam. A voracious reader, he caught the literary bug in his teens, but he continued to be an apprentice imam for the love of it. He once told me about taking over a little mosque in Tripoli that used to play the call to prayer and recitation of the Quran on a cassette for Friday prayers. He disliked this so much that for months he volunteered to recite the Quran and chanted the *adhan* to the worshippers' delight. Due to his excellent language skills and because he had some English, he landed a job as a correspondent with an international news service. And shortly after getting his Islamic studies diploma, he landed a job at the Ministry of Foreign Affairs.

It all came to an abrupt halt, however, when he was sent to jail for being a communist sympathizer in 1978. After his ten years in prison, he was somehow reinstated in his Foreign Ministry job and, hence, resumed his diplomatic career. When I first met Idris in 2001, he was second secretary at the Libyan embassy in New Delhi. He'd had some of his poems translated to English there, and badly so, but I never had the heart to tell him that the translations were poor.

Of course, translation is important to Idris. A few days earlier, he had received a shipment of his Indian-English book, which he personally reprinted in Egypt. He must have been giving away copies of his book to all the foreign reporters and dignitaries who had come to Benghazi in droves since the revolution.

So when I stood at Idris's door, he was on the phone and waved me in. When he hung up, he told me that General Abdul Fattah Younis, chief commander of the revolutionary army, had been kidnapped. Idris's phone kept ringing, at one point he received a call from Mustafa Abdul-Jalil, head of the National Transitional Council—the revolution's veritable George Washington. I was struck by a particular phrase he said to Abdul-Jalil. "We need a statement from the NTC about the Younis situation," Idris said. "We need to translate it so that we can also translate our situation to the world," he added.

Idris really had no time for me that day, so I left him to his work. The following night, after an agonizing wait filled with rumor and random gunfire, Abdul-Jalil made a statement on TV. He reported that anti-Qaddafi fighters from a Jihadi group had kidnapped Younis. His body and those of his companions were found dumped on the outskirts of Benghazi; all had been maimed and burned. It was a shocking revelation that stunned the country.

Things moved quickly thereafter. Tripoli would fall on August 23rd, and I, too, was caught in the euphoria of the victory, for I could hardly believe that the regime that had shaped my life in many ways had finally buckled. People in Tripoli were overjoyed. It seemed the vision of the bride breaking the shackles that bound her in Idris's poem was fulfilled. Benghazi, however, was summarily displaced as the center of the revolution, and Idris was not called to join the new government in Tripoli.

The huge disorder uncorked by the Younis assassination was a troubling sign that would come back to haunt Benghazi and the rest of Libya. The inability to address that crime, among many other signs, indicated that the country lacked a deep language, a language that distinguishes between a mere insurrection and a revolution. The Qaddafi years had left us with little national culture to speak of and very little poetry complex enough to transcend its local origin and unite the country. The country's modern history was too brief to build a sense of the presence or the future upon. The early Qaddafi years, dominated by pan-Arab rhetoric, were followed by decades of the insipid doggerel of his *Green Book*, which sucked the oxygen from the nation's political consciousness. In the meantime, the Islamist tide rumbled underneath, weeding out any sense of humanism outside the fold of radical Islam. Together, Qaddafi's nativism and the Islamists' self-righteousness established a state of derisive anti-intellectualism fueled by arrogance and willful ignorance.

Once the revolution started, Qaddafi's mottos were officially expunged, and in their absence, the impoverishment of the national discourse was laid bare. Yet, to promote national unity, some revolutionaries found themselves repeating phrases from Gaddafi's *Green Book*, not knowing they were the words of the man they had fought to the death. Some saw the need to impose a rule of "iron and fire" to bring order to the country as if that was not what they had lived under. The nation's language was too raw and the terminology of modern governance had no texture in the national consciousness that it could cling to.

The lack of a common language and the violence that was to be post-Qaddafi's Libya acted like two moving walls blocking any sense of vision. Yet in Idris's inadvertent insistence on translation, I continued to see a thread of evanescence, a glimpse of the ineffable that cannot be reached but that can take one a great distance nonetheless. I saw a sense of belonging. What I saw is what Walter Benjamin spoke of in "The Task of the Translator," whereby the translator can captain us to the shores of "pure language" and where translation is "a reference to a thought in the mind of God" (76). I saw a different opportunity for both my native language—in the context of Libya—and for myself, a coming home through translation.

As I'd been trying to say in so many words earlier, translation had always been for me a means to belonging. Through what I had translated so far, I did want to create a shelf of poetry so that nobody can wonder—as Frank O'Hara once mockingly said, "what the poets in Ghana [or the Arab world for that matter] are doing these days" (37). And yes, as it had been noted, I translated poets who perhaps need not have been translated, or whom I've failed to honor fully, if translation is such a thing. Arab poets have been witnesses in Carolyn Forche's sense of the term, where political circumstances pervade the poem and complicate the extent to which the poet can exercise agency. Like Idris, they'd been witnesses for human dignity in the most adverse psychic, political, and economic conditions. Not only did they chronicle their times but also persisted in seeing beyond what they were forced to see. A writer from a country where only the dictator's name was known, I was a branch cut from the tree, as the proverb says, trying to root myself in another language and tradition, a shady suitor asking for the hand of another tribe's beauty. So I brought with me the wisest, bravest, and most gifted men and women of my tribe. They spoke for me and I spoke for them. I carried their interlocutors' questions, and I was the face of the answer. A current of apprehensions and desires flowed through me, and I felt as a river that defines the lands around it.

This process of community-making is at the heart of translation. The irreplaceable translation theorist George Steiner tells us that the first stage in translation is "initiative trust" (312), an investment in the meaningfulness and seriousness of an adverse text . . ." (312). This is a "psychologically hazardous" (312) state that leaves the translator "epistemologically exposed" (312). The philosophical bedrock of this initiative trust is a belief in "the coherence of the world" (312), in "the presence of meaning in very different, perhaps formally, antithetical semantic systems" (312), as well as in "the validity of analogy and parallel" (312) in human interaction.

I recall now the thrill, perhaps known to many translators, of jumping headlong into the first draft of a translation, when one cannot wait to tackle the possibilities, that initial sense of mutual trust between one's abilities and the text translated. The thrill of the first draft, even before the actual translation occurs, is akin to catching a glimpse of the cell at its fullness before it separates, a reproductive moment where the two languages are congealed in the translator's mind, in what Whitman called "the womb cohering." Here, one's past, present, and future are tangled up, and multiple androgynous texts are pregnant and also in need of being birthed through translation. In this unity of potential and merit, of give and take, there is safety and belonging. These are the elemental seeds of thought where the transference of one person's synapses is about to hook itself with another's, a moment where minds are watching the genus of their cells interlace in language.

If I'm leading toward the erotic in my imagery of this union, it is indeed to affirm what Steiner had also argued, which is that Eros and language mesh at every point.

Intercourse and discourse, copula and copulation, are sub-classes of the dominant fact of communication. They arise from the life-need of the ego to reach out and comprehend, in the two vital senses of "understanding" and "containment" of another human being (39).

Sex, adds Steiner, is a "profoundly semantic act" (40). Together with language "they generate the history of self-consciousness, the process . . . whereby we have hammered out the notion of self and otherness . . ." Eros and language/translation "construe the grammar of being" (40).

This remains true, although the other stages of Steiner's definition of translation, such as aggression, sound less peaceful. The aggression stage of translation is, however, "inclusive, incursive, and extractive" (313) action to bring the text home. The translator, like a hunter-gatherer "invades, extracts, and brings home" (314), adds Steiner. Afterwards, we proceed to "incorporation," where we accommodate the new text in the new home, to widen one's grammar and vocabulary. The process definitely "adds to our means" (315) as "we come to incarnate alternative energies and resources of feeling" (315). To incarnate is to live in the flesh of the other. The risk here "is that we may be mastered and made lame by what we have imported" (315), or put on. Then finally, we reach reciprocity where the translation is supposed to "body forth its object" (316).

We are back in the erotic realm but with new anxieties as we experience new ways of looking and reading. The translator notices "an imbalance" where the translation falls "short of the original" (318) perhaps, but where new energies and new "autonomous virtues of the original" (318) text become "more precisely visible" (318) by the translation. What we're talking about then is a manifold relationship where fidelity, like identity, is being created. The translator here "endeavors to restore the balance of forces, of integral presence, which his appropriative comprehension has disrupted" (318). This requires tact so "intensified that it becomes a moral vision" (318).

To be true to another text is not to be an Echo to Narcissus, but to be curious and initiate curiosity. The novelist and art critic John Berger tells us that love is ultimately a kind of curiosity—and there is no richer trail of inquiry than translation, a process that guides us toward the "great longing for the completion of language" (81), to use Benjamin's words. In translation's various phases, we experience longing and its fulfillment being undone by each other, myriad encounters with the ineffable that encapsulate what we live for, and real evidence, in the translated text, that the broken languages of others can find a home within us, a process where longing becomes belonging.

What has excited me about translation since the murkiest days of the Libyan revolution has been the potential of translating to Arabic, of course, something I had not done much before. Fantasies of the many poems that could and needed to be translated have flooded my mind, from the poems of John Clare to Bluegrass and Gospel songs to the ancient Hala poems of India, and the exciting potential that I could experience as I travel back and forth between my two languages.

The energizing element here lies in the opportunity to deepen the roots of contemporary Arabic expression. The young people in my native region indeed sought freedom, but when it came to structuring the new national life, they had few terms to work with. In a recent study of political views in Arab and Muslim societies conducted by John Esposito and Dalia Mogahed, radical Islamists, more even than the secularists, insisted that freedom and freedom of opinion were the most important facets of the society they wished to create (2008). And yet, and predictably so perhaps, when these radical elements got the least bit of power, they went about robbing other citizens of their freedom. In the best cases, they filed lawsuits to ban free expression. And they've moved on to assault, kidnapping, torture, and assassination. What freedom are our radical brothers talking about?

The language of the Arab Spring—the language of chat rooms and Facebook—has not been Arabic per se, much of it is in Latin letters and numbers too, a language devoid of concepts or rootedness. And while it enacts a rebellion against official and religious demagoguery, it also looks and sounds like a hieroglyphics of our impoverishment and despair. Yes, Libya needed to "translate itself" as my friend Idris had said, but what is most needed is to have new worlds translated into us, to explode our language into life.

Why translate? When do languages and literatures engage in translation? Arabic literature is perhaps in its third millennium; it's not a new literature or language seeking to pump itself up through translation. But the conditions in Arab cultural life fit two conditions that give rise to translation that sociolinguist Itamar Even-Zohar had outlined (48). One is that modern Arab literature, especially poetry, is indeed marginal in its society and around the world. When you feel that your own literature is marginal or is becoming closed in and closed-minded, that's when you go out and translate other literatures into your language. Furthermore, Arabic may be a holy language, but it is becoming less respected in its own milieu. It is no longer the language of freedom, invention, or science, no longer the language of tolerance. It is the language of God, and God in our current discourse speaks only of martyrdom, sin, prohibition and shame, terms that are beginning to fall on dead ears. Even for the fundamentalists, many of whom are enrolling their children in English language schools, Arabic is like formaldehyde, there merely to preserve the faith.

Another evident condition for an upsurge of translation, according to Even-Zohar, is a historical turning point. I believe, and still do, that the revolutions in North Africa are indeed a turning point. There is a sense of opportunity rising now with the beginning of the end of Islamism. Amidst the fissures created by the political struggles, new experiences, new aesthetics, tastes, and metaphors are being smuggled into these previously closed societies. Individuals are beginning to rearticulate what they had experienced and what had lain suppressed in them. Even in conservative Libya, new visions of the future are being drawn in colors that had not been seen before.

Translation is instrumental in rearticulation. Through it, a language renews itself testing, speaking, and bodying forth new ideas of what it is to be human. And language renews itself by violating its own parameters. Here, the translator's role is crucial. Benjamin advises the translator to "break through the rotten barriers of his own language . . ." to "extend the frontiers" (82) of one's language. A translator fails, adds Benjamin, when "he holds fast to the state in which his own language happens to be rather than allowing it to be put powerfully in movement by the foreign language" (82).

I realize that these exhilarating descriptions of transforming one's language sound more appropriate for poets than for translators. To that I'll say: show me a poet who has revolutionized his language without translation. Show me a renaissance that was strictly monolingual, that was the product of cultural incest and isolation. Humble and subordinate as he or she is supposed to be in the service of the original text, the translator shares with the modern writer the potential "to create new totalities, to cultivate random appetites" (9) as Edward Said notes. Like a revolutionary poet, the translator can plunge us "into unforeseen estrangements from the habitual" (12), allowing us to experience what had been called defamiliarization, a necessary component of art throughout the ages according to Shklovsky. And like Harold Bloom's strong poets, translators can have ambition, and often do, in finding "through prior [translated] texts an opening for their own totalizing and unique interpretations" (120) of a given culture or social order. They can, even through the least willful of translation, provide us visions they wish to advance.

What I'm saying is that translation contains one of the essential gifts of poetry. The great poets, to me, are those who have a wider sense of what they can see, of what they allow themselves to see, let alone what they allow themselves to feel or empathize with. This is a lesson to us both as poets and as translators. We have to be willing to change what we see and say, to attempt a wider sense of what can be said, seen and felt. Where else can one open up the range of the possible in one's self other than in language, first and foremost? As one translates, one sees the host language playing out itself—how the phrase "into" in English splits like bacteria, and how in Arabic you have to try to find the appropriate single cell/word to place it in because when divided "in" and "to" are heading in different directions. The host language offers more synonyms for your chosen words or less; sometimes it puts its foot down and demands alternate sentence structures. "Everything can be translated," my good friend Anton Shammas once told me. That openness demands that one remain uncertain for a while longer, which is itself a reward. In the wait, perfection flickers like an endless supply of matches, whole and ephemeral, but goodness is possible and evident in the translator's labor and time. In that lack of finality, in our endless attempt to comprehend each other, life roils and kinship weaves us into one another.

Works Cited

Benjamin, Walter. "The Task of the Translator." *Translation Studies Reader.* Ed. Lawrence Venuti. New York: Routledge, 2012.

Esposito, John, and Dalia Mogahed. *Who Speaks for Islam: What Do a Billion Muslims Really Think.* New York: Gallop Press, 2008.

Even-Zohar, Itamar. "The Position of Translated Literature within the Literary Polysystem." *Poetics Today* 11:1 (1990), 45–51.

Mendoza, Plinio Apuleyo and Gabriel García-Márquez. *The Fragrance of Guava.* Trans. Ann Wright. London: Verso, 1983.

O'Hara, Frank. *The Collected Poems of Frank O'Hara*, ed. Donald Allen. Berkeley: University of California, 1971.

Said, Edward. *Beginnings: Intentions and Methods.* New York: Basic Book, 1975.

Sengupta, Mahasweta. "Translation as Manipulation: The Power of Images and Images of Power." *Between Languages and Cultures: Translation and Cross-Cultural Texts*, ed. Anuradha Dingwaney and Carol Maier. Pittsburgh: University of Pittsburgh, 1995. 159–74.

Steiner, George. *After Babel: On Language and Translation*, 3rd ed. Oxford: Oxford University, 1998.

Whitman, Walt. "The Sleepers." http://whitmanarchive.org/published/LG/1891/poems/441

On the Poet's Presence
*Thinking Back, Thinking Forth,
Thinking Darwish and Tagore*

1.

I grew up in Eastern Libya, where people's habits of mind are tied to their vernacular poetry. Like their kin across the border in the Western Desert of Egypt, the inhabitants of Eastern Libya "often punctuated their conversations with short poems" (Abu Lughod 24) called *ghinawat 'alam*. The 'alam poems bear a metonymic relation to given circumstances and are deeply codified in conversation. Anthropologist Lila Abu Lughod, who studied 'alam poetry, found that when she "asked what a poem meant," people "either simply repeated the words or described the type of situation that might elicit that poem" (27).

Using vocabulary particular to the region's dialect and condensed images, the 'alam poems manage to convey meaning despite, and even because of, their density. In this context, the 'alam poem is held in collective ownership, where different emotions have their own poetic hieroglyphs. These hieroglyphs, which could be seen also as allegorical figures, include *yass* (despair), a feeling that the poet must combat constantly, and the *'ain* (the eye), which has a will of its own, weeping over the beloved and grieving over the lost. "Lucky is he who grips his will in hand, / and forgets a loved one who spurned him." There's also the *aziz* (the beloved), who blames, who longs for the poet after too much time has passed, and who spurns and betrays. "I weep not because I miss her beautiful eyes; / it's the betrayal that pangs me."

People do not commonly ask who composed an 'alam song. In fact, querying about the poet's name is often met with a shrug of the shoulders. A poetic phrase or passage does not invite speculations about the poet's intentions or origins but about what the *utterer / user* of the poem means by it. There are times, however, when the lines of poetry recited belong to someone: an author. This is rare, but it makes all the difference. In Eastern Libya, one wants to always know where a person comes from "tribally," even in the cities of Beida and Benghazi. A poet's presence might be noted if it is clear that there is a discrepancy between the author and his tribal background. Otherwise, as 'Aqila notes, it is to be expected that the poet's name would disappear, as would most of the poem's context and historical circumstances (32), and the poem would belong to all its users across the region. This is the normal cycle of oral composition, in which it is also likely that other poets will pick up the poem and improvise upon it.

In Libya, I also witnessed tremendous efforts to place poems in their historical contexts and to recall the often-heroic circumstances that brought about their composition. As a boy, I used to listen to a radio program called "Al-Shi'r wal Shu'ara" ("Poets and Poetry") that was devoted to the classical Arab poetic tradition. Audience members often sent passages of poetry to the program, asking for information about a poem and the circumstances of its writing. The announcer, Muhammad El-Mahdi, would answer these requests by reading a short biography of the poet and providing the occasion of the poem. To me, the moment this clarification occurred amounted to placing the dots on the poem's Arabic letters.

El-Mahdi's explanations asserted that a poem is an act that has a place in history. This is not to say that, once identified, the lines of poetry lost their emblematic or perhaps parabolic power. Rather, when girded by their historical and autobiographical contexts, poems are preserved from drifting into cliché. The specificity of the poet's life and historical circumstances—or what I will call the poet's *presence*—continues to exert a discursive pressure on the poem's use or interpretation. This context is also necessary for establishing the status of the poem. Expressing disappointment when no author could be found for a poem sent his way, El-Mahdi seemed saddened that such a treasure lay unclaimed. Anonymity left a poem incomplete, less meaningful than it could otherwise be.

At stake in these two approaches I experienced in Libya is the question of who gets to claim agency: the utterer/user of the poem, or the person whom we know created it, or both? Though brought up to notice the push and pull between users of poetry who made poems their own and those who wanted to rescue the poet and the poem from anonymity, I spent most of my educational training identifying with neither. Even before hearing of New Criticism or Hermeneutics, I was trained in making the poem/text the center of attention. I read poems to discover complicated class tensions, psychological complexes, notions of gender, ambivalent religious feelings, and insights about a given historical epoch. In that sense, a text is like an artifact from a larger and more enduring whole. The poet's intention is temporary, and the reader's circumstances change. The ideal act of reading, then, was a suppression of both.

Teaching William Blake's "The Chimney Sweeper" from *Songs of Innocence* this summer at the University of Tripoli, I wanted to introduce my students to "irony"—specifically, to dramatic irony as one of the poem's heroes, or what the Russian formalists called "the dominant device." The other hero was the rampant exploitation that capitalism had fostered and religion's contribution to the continuation of such oppression. And of course, there was the five-year-old chimneysweeper likely to die soon of black lung, whose story is being told by the slightly older, naive speaker. Instead I found myself thinking of Blake and his presence in the poem. I needed him to understand the gesture his poem made. How did Blake go about getting himself to the point of writing the poem? What did the poet want to provoke or invoke by writing this poem? "Who is the sayer of this poem, and what was the occasion?" I found myself saying to my class in Tripoli in homage to El-Mahdi.

2.

The relationship between the poet and his or her poem, and how that relationship facilitates the cultural resonance of a poem, is complicated, to say the least. This process is layered even when the poet and the reader are from the same culture and speak the same language. In none of the schools of Anglo-American poetry (Romanticism, Modernism, Confessionalism, postmodern postlanguage) does the poet forego the potential to connect with or impact the reader. Experimental poems may evoke alienation, but estranging the reader is at most a technique. Some postlanguage American poets argue that the difficult nature of their poems is meant to enliven the reader's experience through defamiliarization, among other approaches. Here is how the poet Ron Silliman described the techniques of his fellow language poets and what they hoped to achieve:

By the creation of non-referring structures (Coolidge, Di Palma, Andrews), disrupting of context (Grenier, Dejasu), forcing meanings in upon themselves until they cancel out (Watten . . . , Palmer). By effacing one or more elements of referential language (. . . the Russian Futurists), the balance within the words shifts, redistributes. (118)

We note here that Silliman is careful to "redistribute" the balance after it "shifts," and does not do away with balance completely. The disorienting effects in which the poet's language ranges beyond ordinary syntax and sense-making are meant to lead to a new balance or a shared "field of action," to use William Carlos Williams's term (56). Thinking "with the poem and not with a preconceived master plan, and going where the poem led him" (Mariani 540) is how Paul Mariani explains W. C. Williams's process, whereby the poet is a guide on a difficult journey with his reader as they slog through the dissonance of the modern experience, assembling meaning together.

In that way, most avant-garde poets share a similar outlook with the oral poets of my native region—they and their readers rely on a shared context. The poet assumes he is speaking to fellow citizens with whom he shares a common tongue and contingency. The 'alam poet sometimes addresses his foes, whom he expects do understand his context and would want to put an effort into deciphering his complex images and allusions. The avant-garde artist similarly anticipates that our shared context would spur us to put a great deal of effort into deciphering her complex thoughts and filling in the blanks in her ellipses.

In other words, attempts at the elliptical and open-ended are inherently local, as they emerge from and speak to a given context. Like installation or performance art, some forms of experimental poetry that aspire toward renewal are bound in the collaborative and circumstantial convergence of their practitioners. Dada, surrealism, the New York School, the Beats, the two branches of language poetry that were also divided between the two coasts, and Negritude—all depend on a local context, and much is missed when that context is lacking. Similarly the 'alam poem remains a phenomenon of Eastern Libya. Even after one hundred years of national unification, the 'alam has not crossed beyond its region and has never quite entered the city, but has remained on the outskirts, always ready to run back to its low-slung Green Mountains, its native ground. When recited in the city, it's like a wild herb freshly plucked and fragrant with the rawness and delicacy of the outdoors. A plant that no one has planted.

Certainly, postlanguage poets claim their poems, but it's difficult to connect that claim with a self responsible for the ideas, emotions, and experiences relayed. In fact, absenting the self, or transcending it, is part of the post-language project. Without a subject claimant, we are asked to make poetry itself the owner of these lines. For the 'alam poet, absent and nameless as he or she may be, the adherence to a given meter in his or her poem and the treatment of familiar themes pave the way for the work's insertion into poetry. It's much harder, however, for the language/experimental poet, whose project may be even antipoetic, to remember what the poetry is attempting to do. We are tempted to think here of how such self-less poems could be used.

How would one, for example, describe the work of Kenneth Goldsmith, as interesting as it is conceptually? Are there any lines to remember or substantial ideas that can be perceived as his? He is known as the poet who turned the *New York Times* edition of September 11, 2001, into a book (of poems, perhaps), and he is also known for his trilogy of *Weather*, *Traffic*, and *Sports*, where radio reports are transcribed and edited in a particular manner to perhaps create total immersion, circularity, and repetition to generate poetic effect or induce narrative pleasure. In *Day*, the absence of the tragic event allows the poet to project his grief and loss and thus make his statement. The fact that he actually transcribed the day's edition himself into one book constitutes an act of dedication and even exaction by him. Tension is created with the transcription, moving page-by-page rather than article-by-article. It asserts the poet's presence in his act of reading and processing. But how do we weigh *Day* as a response? In essence, it's an attempt to capture a world that existed before the bombings, with many hints of a lost innocence perhaps, and indications that the world was changed utterly—to use Yeats' line—by the 9/11 events. The preservation of this state of not-knowing stands as an act of elegy and consolation for the poet's fellow New Yorkers.

But in retrospect, we cannot fail to see the sentimentality both in the statement made—the assertion of innocence—as an aspect of melodrama and in the poet's act of sitting down to transcribe the whole edition, an act of suffering and labor undertaken for the whole city. It's very difficult not to see through that element of the gesture. Goldsmith's most recent work, *Seven American Deaths and Disasters*, revisits the assassination of JFK, RFK, John Lennon, and other tragic deaths. Made up of transcripts of radio broadcasts as the incidents unfolded, the book attempts to capture people's shock to evoke a state of unknowing that characterizes an earlier version of America. Using what may be a revolutionary textual technique, Goldsmith's works are deeply conventional. And that conventionality may be highlighted by the poet's absence or what may have been seen as an avant-garde technique.

A more revolutionary work, perhaps, *Sunset Debris* by Ron Silliman is made up entirely of questions. Here's a passage:

> Is it like this in dream? Can you smell the rain? What was the reason for the suitcase of doughnuts? Was that government grammar? Why is that window made out of blue glass? Are those sea birds or birds of prey? Which shore is Africa, which is Spain? Is that what one would call a high sky? How can I know that what you feel is pain, orgasm, satisfaction? What are you thinking? (Silliman, 2002)

It would exhaust me to try to find a sequential or symmetrical arc to the questions or determine if the book adds up to an argument, or even a persona, in the way that Beckett's novels do. Though full of beautiful and evocative language, *Sunset Debris* is not a book that I could read in one sitting, or could read for more than a few snippets at a time. A writerly text, it is a perfect prompt for writing (perhaps non-experimental texts), inviting us to fill the void left by its unanswered and unclaimed questions.

And I suspect, too, that Goldsmith's works will in due time begin to have a talismanic life. People will speak of them and not necessarily read them. (A scholar of experimental writing once told me, confidentially, that she likes hearing experimental writers talking about their work more than she likes reading the works themselves). As a New York City book, I can imagine Goldsmith's *Day* gaining sentimental value, to preserve memory, a testament of collective suffering, but not being read. Like the 'alam songs, experimental works are indeed useful.

3.

If poetic experimentation and trenchantly local oral poetry do not travel well, the poets of our modern age have been on the move, crossing borders and languages and cobbling together audiences from various parts of the globe. The twentieth century has been a century of great European and Latin American poets. But when I think of poets who stepped outside their linguistic milieus and tried to speak for, and speak to, multiple constituencies, it's Rabindranath Tagore and Mahmoud Darwish who come to mind. Not even part of Western literature, and yet arguably among the best-known poets of the twentieth century, Tagore and Darwish sought to be heard by people outside their "national" milieus. The pressure their life stories and their poetic personae exert on their poems enriches our reading of their poems and our sense of poetry as a vital art form.

Poets from colonized or occupied territories, Darwish and Tagore had to address the powerlessness and lowly status of their nations. Their poetic projects attempt to re-negotiate this perception and place them as speakers for their people and as unique individuals at the same time. They are what could be called "identifying poets," to use a term coined by the Scottish critic Robert Crawford. Identifying poets are poets "who have made for themselves identities which let them be identified with, restate, or even renovate the identity of a particular territory" (Crawford 1). In the identifying poet's work, we can discern the formation of an "'I,' which is somewhat removed from the 'I' of the authorial producer. . . . It is not a piece of individual soul-bearing so much as the creation of a textual self" (3–4). The identifying poet's persona is attuned to the world and "depends less on a looking-in than on a looking-out" (12). As such, it allows the identifying poet to position himself as an active agent in negotiating how cultural and even psychological territories are drawn.

To be sure, Crawford's use of the term "territory" in his definition of the identifying poet is largely geographical. The poet creates a textual self that allows him to speak from both sides of the boundaries of self and culture, a presence that girds the poems with necessary context, lest the poem be lost in the oblivion of poetry or in the echo chamber of a shared cause. In the cases of Darwish and Tagore, the poetic "identifying" persona stands on the poet's own shoulders and feeds on his history and experience. And it gives forth poems that unfold into deeper layers of meaning as we dig deeper into their contexts and occasions, poems that become monumental for their being rooted in self and history.

4.

Born in a village that was razed by the Israeli army in 1948 and living as a present absentee in his native land and then as an exile for most of his life, Darwish acknowledges that the confrontation with the Israeli occupier who threatens the lives of all Palestinians has been a constant presence in his life—a source of poetic energy as well as an impediment to poetic creation. "My early interest in poetry developed with my realization that I am a victim of some form of military and political aggression," he states (Darwish 1971, 244). Yet to write poetry "that focuses and fascinates the reader's mind" (377), poetry that is not devoted to the Palestinian cause had been one of Darwish's lifelong aims.

This irreconcilable strain between poetry of political contingency and the dream of "universal," non-contingent poetry can be detected very early in Darwish's career. In "To the Reader," published in 1964, the eighteen-year-old Darwish apologizes for writing about the political conditions that have driven him to anger. The assumption here is that anger would not have been part of his poetry had he a choice in the matter:

To the Reader
Black irises in my heart
    and on my lips . . . flame.
From what forest did you come to me
    O crosses of anger?
I have allied myself to sorrows,
    I have shaken hands with banishment and hunger
My hands are anger,
my mouth is anger
the blood of my arteries a juice of anger.
O my reader,
    do not ask me to whisper,
    do not expect musical delight.
                                (2005, 15)

Where did this anger come from, the poet asks, and why was he burdened with it? These questions suggest that the poet was once in a state that precluded anger and that anger is not his ordinary nature. We as readers, however, wonder when that peaceful state could have existed for Darwish and his people between 1948, the year Israel came into being and the Palestinian dispossession began, and the time of the poem's writing. Until that point, no such precaution was heard of or deemed necessary in twentieth-century Palestinian poetry. We are left to wonder what place the poet wishes to carve out for himself by bemoaning his unwanted anger. He states that he would rather write love poetry—full of positive emotions, serene meditations, and lyricism—than address the causes of his people's plight and anger.

Couched in apology, the poem is not without coyness. The poem is short enough that it can indeed be whispered to explain the poet's intention and dilemma. The poet is clearly being ironic when he tells us not to expect musical delight, for the poem is precisely measured and exquisitely rhymed in Arabic. Fulfilling his artistic obligations, the poet asserts his presence, expressing a dilemma that he may have known would preoccupy him throughout his career—mainly, a desire to write poems that do not arise from a fateful anger or, later, exile, siege, and betrayal.

Another poem, written in 1964, "Identity Card," has been a fan favorite throughout the Arab world, one that audiences frequently asked Darwish to read at his recitations. The poem was made into a popular song and has been an unofficial Arab nationalist anthem for decades. Yet it is one that Darwish never read in public after leaving Israel/Palestine in 1970:

> Write it down!
> I am an Arab
> employed with fellow workers at a quarry.
> I have eight children.
> I earn their bread,
> clothes and books
> out of these rocks.
> I do not beg for charity at your doors.
> Nor do I kneel
>   on your marble floor.
>   So does this anger you?
> So Now!
>   Record at the top of the first page:
>   I do not hate people
>   nor do I steal.
>   But if I become hungry
>   I will eat my robber's flesh.
> Beware then, beware of my hunger
> *and my anger!*
>   (2005, 80–84)

The poem's speaker, whose life details bear a remarkable resemblance to those of Darwish's own father, was expelled from his village, lost his farm, ended up working in a quarry, and fathered eight children. The angry speaker has suffered patiently and remained proud despite living under occupation. But now he draws a red line: he will not beg from the one who stole his land, and he will fight his usurper to fend off hunger; indeed, he will turn into a cannibal if need be. The speaker's last words, "Beware of my hunger and my anger," (2005, 84) irrevocably intertwine these two conditions. This poem provides a basis for the anger expressed in "To the Reader."

Why, then, has Darwish refused to recite the poem in public since he left Palestine/Israel? During one packed recitation in Beirut, a member of the audience kept saying "Write it down, / I am an Arab," asking that Darwish read the poem. Fed up with the repeated request, Darwish shot back at the listener, "Write it down yourself!" and went on to read a different poem (al-Sayyid 2008, 7).

According to Darwish, the circumstances sparking the poem occurred when he was placed under partial house arrest in Haifa in the mid-1960s. "'Write it down: I am Arab.' I said that to a government official," Darwish explained. "I said it in Hebrew to provoke him, but when I said it in Arabic (in the poem) the Arab audience in Nazareth was electrified" (Darwish 2007a, 180). The poem, a dramatic monologue addressed to Darwish's detainers, continues as a translation of what Darwish would have said to the Israeli policemen in Hebrew.

"Identity Card" was written within the first two decades of the state of Israel, a time when the word "Palestine" was banned, and Palestinians were merely Arabs. The electrified audience gathered in a Nazareth cinema in 1964 asked Darwish to repeat the poem six times, thrilled with the way the poem turns *Arab* from a derogatory term uttered to humiliate a dispossessed person into a declaration of dignified humanity before the Israelis, who confiscated their lands and designated them third-class citizens.

In Beirut in the 1970s and thereafter, the refrain—"Write it down, / I am an Arab"—took on a different resonance, devoid of the specific context in which Darwish wrote the poem. "Write it down, / I am an Arab!" became an anthem expressing Arab national pride, as opposed to the defiance of subjugation and racism that the poet had meant it to be. Darwish explains, "the Jews call the Palestinian an Arab, and so I shouted in my tormentor's face 'Write it down, I am an Arab!' Does it make sense then for me to stand before a hundred million Arabs saying 'I am an Arab'? No, I'll not read the poem" (al-Qaissī 2008, 13).

Here, Darwish suggests that poems do target different audiences and serve as specific rhetorical gestures or even as political messages that should not be taken out of their historical contexts. In other words, poems do not necessarily have "universal" messages, because they emerge during different contingencies with different interlocutors. The poet imposes his presence on the poem, refuses to grant his poem permission to travel beyond his intended meaning. Audiences read the poem as they wished, but in the lore of "Identity Card," the poet's disapproval of such readings casts a shadow on the poem and becomes part of the reading experience.

Thirty-six years later, in 2000, Darwish published a book-length poem titled *Jidariya* (*Mural*) to wide acclaim in the Arab world. A few years before, Darwish had told a documentary filmmaker that he wished for the Palestinian trauma to end, just so that he would know how good a poet he is (Bitton, 1997). The poet continued to suspect that his work, attached as it was to Palestine and the Palestinians, could only be judged on the basis of that attachment. He longed for an opportunity to demonstrate his skills in the daylight of artistic judgment alone. Darwish wrote *Mural* in France shortly after he survived major heart surgery. He was briefly in a coma and had a near-death experience:

> Nothing ails me at the gate of Judgment day,
> not time or emotions.
> I feel neither the lightness of things
> nor the heaviness of premonitions . . .
> There is no nothingness here
> in the no-here, in the no-time,
> of no existence.
>   (Darwish 2006, 442–43)

The world is white in "this sky of the absolute" (443). The speaker suspects he had died previously because he "know[s] this vision" (443) and knows he is heading somewhere he does not know. From this nexus of oblivion and erasure emerges poetic renewal and possibility:

> Maybe
>
> I am still alive somewhere and I know
> what I want to be . . .

> One day I will be what I wish to be,
> one day I will be an idea, carried by a sword
> to free a wasteland with a book in hand,
> as if it were rain falling on a mountain aching,
> aching with the grass bursting through its soil,
> somewhere where power had not won
> nor where justice has become a fugitive.
> One day I will be what I wish to be . . .
> one day I will be a poet . . .
> One day I will be what I wish to be.
>
> (446–47)

Darwish's repetition of "One day I will be what I wish to be" vacillates between chant and plaint; the hope it seeks is singed by a long struggle with despair. Most inspiring, and also humbling, in this passage is Darwish's declaration that he wishes to be a poet one day. What horizons, aesthetic or otherwise, could this poet be seeking if he thinks he has never been a poet to begin with? Darwish's presence is necessary to appreciate the depth of this passage, given when it was said and by whom, as Muhammad al-Mahdi would have reported on his radio program. Context is important and enriching, as it adds a dramatic layer and a great amount of pathos to the rich lyricism, which indeed could stand alone but is now complemented by a rich landscape of signification.

Implied in the sketch of the new poet Darwish would be are the whiteness (of death) that he wished to fill with his poetry, the whiteness of the blank page (the pages he filled with poetry erased and forgotten), and the whiteness of the identity card on which his fate had been inscribed. All the poet needed to do in this new space/place, as the nurse instructed him, was to "remember your name to keep it safe. / Do not betray it, / pay no mind to the banners of the tribes. / Be a good friend to your name." (2006, 447). His muse at the time, she reminds him to remember his presence, to insist on the dignity of his person and his artistic project.

5.

Rabindranath Tagore's career is so multi-faceted, it is difficult to know where to begin with him. Writing poetry, fiction, essays, and drama, Tagore helped shape Bengali modernity with a wide-ranging body of work that positioned him as an educator, cultural critic, and rebel. Tagore's initial appearance on the literary scene in Bengal in 1875 received genuine enthusiasm, though it was in fact a prank. Fourteen at the time, Tagore invented a classical poet named Bhanisimha and wrote poems that were so well contrived they passed as genuine articles. Critics lauded the newly discovered ancient bard who ended up being the subject of a doctoral dissertation in Germany in the late 1880s (Robinson and Dutt 12; Krishna 71; Thomson 10).

The enthusiasm that met Tagore's ploy was not entirely due to his genius. Bengal was at the center of India's renaissance at the time, which launched the struggle against British colonialism. Long settled into a habitual veneration of their history, Indians turned toward their literary heritage—some of it discovered by Orientalists—as a basis for their claim to be among the world's nations. It was important to try to match the English at their literary skills. Writers such as Toru Dutt, Henry Durozio, Sri Auribindo, and Michael Madhusudan Dutt attempted that. It was equally important to prove that India has produced outstanding literary works throughout the ages.

Tagore was aware of this anxiety, and perhaps it was inevitable for a young poet in a household of poets to use this anxiety to distinguish himself. Clearly, by duping those he wished to impress, Tagore signaled open disregard for their taste. The classical tradition was so steeped in convention, so unoriginal, that a precocious fourteen-year-old could easily imitate it, he seems to say. But the mastery is ultimately a deep acknowledgement of that tradition. Tagore's youthful prank positioned him as both an inheritor of a literary tradition and a rebel intent on reshaping it.

Soon thereafter, and writing under his own name, Tagore takes up his mission. In the poem "Unending Love," he writes, "My spellbound heart has made and remade the necklace of songs / that you take as a gift" (1985, 49). The songs are to be cherished because of their "merging" with "the songs of every poet past and forever" (49). The love the poet-speaker expresses is only as strong as his ability to weave the countless loves that preceded it.

The poet's love is made of "old love, / but in shapes that renew and renew forever." It is "heaped before" the beloved's feet. "It has found its end in you, / The love of all man's days both past and forever." While there is no claim for uniqueness, it is the poet who takes the old poems and old love and shapes them anew. It all comes through him in a grand act of appropriation. But unlike someone reciting an 'alam poem, Tagore is not merely using the old poetry; he is assembling it, shaping it, and carrying it forward.

In another early act of appropriation, Tagore's poem "Meghaduta" bears the same title as a poem by the ancient poet Kalidasa,[1] whose original is in the voice of a devotee of Kubera, the god of wealth. After being exiled for a year to central India, the poet-speaker of Kalidasa's poem addresses a cloud and implores it to reach his beloved. The cloud crosses the geography of India, cataloging her people, her flora and fauna, her gods and myths, making the poem an idyll that ties these impressions of the land with the noblest human emotions.

In his "Meghaduta," Tagore praises his predecessor Kalidasa:

> In a single day the heart-held grief of a thousand years
> Of pining, long repressed tears,
> Broke time's bonds, and seems to have poured down . . .
>   and drenched your noble stanzas.
>
>   (1985, 50)

As in "Unending Love," we encounter the idea that Kalidasa's poem is made of layers of sounds and feelings. But what was in the poet's verses before they were drenched by other voices? Tagore never quite clarifies. He does suggest, however, that Kalidasa simply received his poem and his poem did not come into being until the echoes of other lovers entered it and gave it form.

Tagore goes on to interrogate his predecessor, asking him several rhetorical questions, partly to state his own poetic agenda. He writes:

> Did every exile in the world that day
> Raise his head, clasp his hands, face his beloved's home
> And sing to the clouds one and the same
> Song of yearning? Did each lover ask a fresh, unfettered cloud
> To carry on its wings a tearful message of love
> To the distant window where his beloved
> Lay wretched on the ground with clothes disordered
> And hair unplaited and weeping eyes?
> Did your music, O poet, carry all their songs
> As you journeyed in your poem through land after land
> Over many days and nights
> Toward the lonely object of your love?
>   (1985, 50)

Tagore's questions are stacking the deck against Kalidasa. He's inviting us to doubt that Kalidasa's poem could achieve all these goals and, in essence, asking us to move beyond the ancient bard. Reading Kalidasa's poem again, Tagore's poet-speaker is ready to strike on his own. His mind "leaves the room, / travels on a free-moving cloud, flies far and wide" (1985, 51).

Tagore can't help but take Kalidasa to task once more. Ending his poem with a wish for reconciliation, Kalidasa had addressed the cloud that gave him his journey, saying, "May you never be separated even for a moment / from your beloved lightning" (Kalidasa 21). In response, Tagore in his "Meghaduta" is "sleepless half the night, asking / Who has cursed us like this? Why the gulf?" (1985, 52) between lover and beloved. "Why do we aim so high only to weep when thwarted? / Why does love not find its true path?" Tagore adds.

By the end of Tagore's poem, we realize that he has been engaged in an almost point-by-point *tessera* (a completion based on antithesis) of Kalidasa's *Meghaduta*. Tessera, a term resuscitated by Harold Bloom, refers to a process whereby

> the poet antithetically "completes" his precursor's work, by so reading the parent poem as to retain its terms but to mean them in another sense, as though the precursor had failed to go far enough. (1973, 66)

The fact of separation is unshakeable, and while Kalidasa's poem provides an imaginative leap at assuaging it, it does little to lift "the curse" within which Tagore feels trapped. Tagore's poetry deconstructs his predecessor's work and introduces a new anxiety that shows both his command and transcendence of his predecessor's work. He positions himself as the beginning of a new literature fit for a new age.

Much time and circumstance pass between the poems above and the poem I'll discuss now. In the forty years between, Tagore became the leading poet in Bengal and indeed all of India. He travelled to England in 1912, at the age of fifty-two, for medical treatment, and there met Ezra Pound and W. B. Yeats. A sheaf of his translations of his own poems, edited and introduced by Yeats, became *Gitanjali*, a book of powerful, seemingly devotional poems that earned Tagore the Nobel Prize in 1913. Tagore hardly stopped travelling after that, and his growing fame took him everywhere. *Gitanjali* and much of Tagore's poetry that was translated into European languages fostered the notion of him as a poet-guru from the East. It was a persona that Western audiences were willing to accept and that Tagore did not refuse. Tagore believed Eastern spirituality could ameliorate the effects Western materialism and destructive nationalism had on the rest of the world. He also believed that Western rationality and science could help the "East" recover from its poverty, sectarianism, and caste and ethnic divisions. In *Gitanjali* and later works, Tagore expresses a yearning for connection that remains bold and affecting. Tagore's drive to travel and network, his practice of ubiquity, and his desire to infuse people with awareness of events and happenings around the world arose from an existential need. "If I do not apprehend what is outside of me, I do not feel myself either. The stronger the sense of the world outside, the more robust is the sense of one's own inner being" (Tagore 2001, 293). Awareness of the outside world, be it present or past, helps the poet locate the self, and indeed positions him to compose his poetry. He can only know his own feelings through the tableau of a wide range of feelings and experiences happening around him, be they near or far. Tagore traveled all over the Americas, Europe, and the Middle East. He went to Japan and tried to convince the Japanese to quit their racist nationalism. He met with Mussolini and tried to do the same.

The onset of World War II felt like a personal defeat to Tagore, having seen it coming, and having warned against racist nationalism everywhere he went. His grief is best witnessed in "Bombshell," a poem that only Tagore could have written:

> The sinking sun extends its late afternoon glow.
>   The wind has dozed away.
>   An ox-cart laden with paddy-straw bound
> For far-off Nadiya market crawls across the empty open land,
>   Calf following, tied on behind
> Over towards the Rajbamsi quarter. Banamali Pandit's
>   Eldest son sits
> On the edge of a tank, fishing all day.
>   From overhead comes the cry
>   Of wild duck making their way
>   From the dried-up river's
> Sandbanks towards the Black Lake in search of snails.
>   Along the side of newly-cut sugar-cane
> Fields, in the fresh air of trees washed by rain,
>   Through the wet grass,

> Two friends pass
>   Slowly, serenely—
>   They came on a holiday,
> Suddenly bumped into each other in the village.
>   One of them is newly married—the delight
> Of their conversation seems to have no limit.
>   All around in the maze
> Of winding paths in the wood, bhati-flowers
>   Have come into bloom,
> Their scent dispensing the balm
>   Of Caitra. From the jarul-trees nearby
> A koel-bird strains its voice in dull, demented melody.
>
>   A telegram arrives:
> "Finland pounded by Soviet bombs."
>
> (1985, 118–19)

The form of the poem immediately implies the imbalance of its content. A heavy, laden stanza almost dripping with life precedes a spare couplet with devastating news. By the time we read the last couplet, we are forced to read the poem again to seek clues, as if on a crime scene, to absorb the shocking conclusion. Was anything indicative of the oncoming shelling? Was the natural scene in Bengal trying to tell us something about what was happening a world away, and if so, what was it? We see only scenes of slow movement: a bullock-drawn cart "crawls," two friends pass each other slowly, and a boy sits fishing all day. The bhati flowers seem as giddy as Wordsworth's daffodils, as do the friends who meet unexpectedly, one of whom has just gotten married. The koel-bird's dull and demented melody does ring with foreshadowing, but we cannot be certain.

In this closed world, the birds' cries prove to be false alarms, a trick of our own minds that forces us to face our desire to connect our foregone displacements. To remain at rest in such a place is to admit despair and helplessness. The news from Finland informs us that another country has been drawn into World War II, a conflict that Tagore anticipated and vigorously opposed. In Tagore's refusal to comment on the impact of this devastating news, we are pervaded by the disappointment of a man's work gone to naught. Tagore's presence in the poem is the shock and anguish that fills the white space between the two stanzas. Recognizing the poet's presence, we too are trapped in the disappointment and pain of our inability to be in two places and to transport the peace of one place to another.

6.

In his short story "La Busca de Averroes" ("Averroes's Search"), the great Argentine writer Jorge Luis Borges imagines the difficulty that Averroes, the famed Islamic philosopher, faced in translating Aristotle's *Poetics* because he had never seen live drama. A traveler who had gone to China tries to describe to Averroes a dramatic performance he had seen there:

> One evening, the Muslim merchants of Sin-I Kalal conducted me to a house of painted wood in which many persons lived.... There were people sitting on the floor as well, and also on a raised terrace. The people on this terrace were playing the tambour and the lute—all, that is, save some fifteen or twenty who wore crimson masks and prayed and sang and conversed among themselves. These masked ones suffered imprisonment, but no one could see the jail; they rode upon horses, but the horse was not to be seen; they waged battle, but the swords were of bamboo; they died, and then they walked again ...
>
> No one understood, no one seemed to want to understand. Abu-al-Hasan, in some confusion, swerved from the tale he had been telling them into inept explanation. Aiding himself with his hands, he said: "Let us imagine that someone shows a story instead of telling it.... It was something like that that the persons on the terrace showed us that evening."
>
> "Did these persons speak?" asked Faraj.
>
> "Of course they did," said abu-al-Hasan, now become the apologist for a performance that he only barely recalled.... They spoke and sang and gave long boring speeches!"
>
> "In that case," said Faraj, "there was no need for twenty persons. A single speaker could tell anything, no matter how complex it might be." (Borges 73–74)

I thought about Borges's story as I was writing this essay and as it was becoming clear that I was siding with the poet's presence over his erasure or absence. Was I making the same mistake as my ancestor Averroes, missing out on a great art form? Perhaps, but I doubt it. Averroes's is a great story, and it is there to remind us never to take an absolute stance on any form of art, if we wish to be fully alive and receptive as poets and human beings.

The 'alam poems remind us that poetry can move thoughts further and can ennoble emotions by affirming them in ways we could not express. But with Muhammad El-Mahdi as an inspiration, too, it was not difficult to create a myth of Darwish and Tagore as genies who managed to burst out of their respective lamps of colonial obscurity and forge, out of the solitude of their craft, responsive and enduring works of art. Both have much to teach us about the evolution of poetic agency in the world today, where many of the poets we read come from places where poetry takes on cultural and political duties in addition to providing lyric insight and musical delight. Such duties could not have been fulfilled in the cases of Darwish and Tagore without the poets claiming a place in poetry. Granted, poems should stand alone, should be able to say what they say, like photographs, perhaps to convey their content. But do we lose anything in a poem when the poet's presence or story fulfills other contexts? What's wrong with a poem that conveys a life lived as well as the circumstance? There's nothing wrong, of course. In fact, our knowledge of the poet's presence provides enriching and sometimes necessary dimensions to fully read the poems. As to the 'alam poetry of my region, which has lived without a poet's presence, it has managed to finds its musical way to people's ears and to address their sorrow and despair for millennia. Not many poems can easily claim that. But perhaps remembering our names as Darwish's nurse commanded him, claiming our poems, and positioning our poetic projects from a standpoint of ambition and relevance is use enough to us as readers and poets.

Notes

1. Kalidasa's biography is in dispute. It is reported that he lived somewhere between the fourth and first centuries BC.

Works Cited

Abu Lughod, Leila. *Veiled Sentiments.* Berkeley: University of California, 1993.
Aquila, Ahmad Yusuf. *Ghanawat al-'Alam,* vol. 1. Benghazi: Dar Al-Ibl lil-Nashr wal Tawzia, 2008.
Bitton, Simmon. *Mahmoud Darwish: Et la terre, comme la langue* [*As the Land Is the Language*] (video recording), in coproduction with France 3, Point du Jour; a film by Simone Bitton and Elias Sanbar; Simon Bitton, director, Mireille Abramovici, editor, 1997.

Bloom, Harold. *The Anxiety of Influence*. New York: Oxford University, 1973.
Borges, Jorge Luis. *Aleph and Other Stories*. Translated by Andrew Hurley. New York: Penguin Books, 2004.
Crawford, Robert. *Identifying Poets: Self and Territory in Twentieth-Century Poetry*. Edinburgh: Edinburgh University, 1994.
Darwish, Mahmoud. *Shai a'an al-Watan*. Beirut: Dar al-A'awda, 1971.
Darwish, Mahmoud. *Al-A'amal al-Jadida*. Beirut: Riyadh al-Rayyes, 2006.
Darwish, Mahmoud. *Al-A'amal al-Ula*. Beirut: Riyadh al-Rayyes, 2005.
Darwish, Mahmoud. *Dhakirat lil-Nissyan*. Beirut, Riyyad al-Rayyes, 2007.
Dutta, Krishna and Robinson, Andrew. *Rabindranath Tagore: The Myriad-Minded Man*. New York: St. Martin's Press, 1996.
Kalidasa. "The Meghaduta." Translated by M. McComas. http://chl.anu.edu.au/languages/sanskrit/meghaduta_english.pdf
Marianni, Paul. *The Poet and His Critics: A New World Naked*. New York: W. W. Norton, 1990.
Al-Qaissi, Yahya. "Min Hayat Darwish fi 'Amman," *Al-Quds Al-Arabi*, "Mulhaq Khass" (special supplement on Mahmoud Darwish), September 20–21, 2008, pp. 9–11.
Al-Sayyid, Nazim. "Mahmoud Darwish fi Khaymatihi al-Beirutia," *Al-Quds Al-Arabi*, "Mulhaq Khass" (special supplement on Mahmoud Darwish), September 20–21, 2008, pp. 6–8.
Silliman, Ron. "Introduction to 'The Dwelling Place: 9 Poets'," *Alcheringa*, vol. 1, no. 2, 1975.
Silliman, Ron. *Sunset Debris*. Ubu ebook, 2002.
Tagore, Rabindranath. *Selected Poems*. Translated by William Radice. New York, Penguin, 1985.
Tagore, Rabindranath. *Selected Writings on Literature and Language*. Edited by Sisir Kumar Das and Sukata Chaudhuri. New Delhi: Oxford University Press, 2001.
Thompson, Edward John. *Rabindranath Tagore: His Life and Work*. London: Association Press (Y.M.C.A.), 1921.
Williams, William Carlos. *Selected Essays*. New York: New Directions, 1958.

Resisting the Lapse into Monologue
On the Poetics of Bilingualism
in American Poetry

Within the first twenty lines of "The Waste Land," T. S. Eliot demonstrates that he is a practitioner of the beliefs he would later state in his essay, "Tradition and the Individual Talent." His intertextual exhibition aims to show that the poet does indeed have "in his bones . . . the whole literature of Europe." In the essay, he declares that the literature of Europe is linked in a traceable fashion (from the present to Homer) and, as a body of thought, composes "the mind of Europe." By the end of the first stanza (including the prefatory note and the dedication to Pound), Eliot uses five languages (English, Latin, Greek, Italian, and German). Expecting his readers to be acquainted with the mind of Europe in its various linguistic manifestations, Eliot provides no English translations of his borrowings. To apprehend the poem, readers have to look up these passages and, in effect, become actively engaged with "their" larger European heritage.

This use of other languages in Modernist poetry reflects an impulse that motivated the Anglo-American Modernists, mainly the desire to gather a scattered Western culture under a unified umbrella of a shared heritage. Of course, that the project was exclusive by virtue of its rigorous requirements meant that it could unify only a small band of elite intellectuals. In the *Cantos,* Ezra Pound displayed a similar technique in attempting to create an all-encompassing poetic vision to point a new direction for Western culture. Pound's project was also a multilingual one, and he too provided no translations of its Latin, Chinese, Greek, and Italian borrowings.

Writers in the postmodern era have abandoned such large-scale cultural projects. In contemporary American poetry, elitist prioritizing of a shared background in Greek and Latin has petered out. Latin still flashes here and there; Greek is usually accompanied by translation. Yet, American poetry is becoming more and more multilingual through the diverse native usages of its bilingual practitioners. This multilingualism is most evident in the writings of minority or immigrant poets. These bilingual borrowings are not meant to unify a diversified culture but to express the poet's identity and perhaps aid the poet's struggling subculture from being subsumed.

Various communities throughout U.S. history have tried to maintain distinct linguistic cultural identities within the American mainstream. These current efforts, however, differ from earlier ones. No longer coming from Europe alone, recent immigrants have more cultural differences to bridge as they negotiate the possibilities of assimilation. Furthermore, America's history of racial strife, the racial undertones of its patriotic rhetoric, and the existence of an obdurate elite establishment have contributed to making American nationalism an uninviting prospect. Also, technological innovations have made it possible for immigrants to maintain closer bonds to their native cultures. A central paradox of the present American experience has to be that as the world becomes increasingly homogenized in its modes of production and even in its tastes, it is also more possible for people to actually take their cultures with them wherever they go. Native languages constitute the most valued possessions immigrant cultures attempt to hold on to.

Consequently, a number of bilingual American poets have displayed ambivalence toward English. Latino American poets, mainly Chicano/a and Puerto Rican, have expressed positions toward the English language similar to those expressed by "commonwealth" writers in their critique of British colonialism. Puerto Ricans in the mainland United States have "sustained ambiguous attitudes toward the use of English, the language of the oppressor, which is at times their own first language" (Mohr 100). Similarly, the imperialist nature of U.S. historical relations with Mexico still resonates with Chicano/a poets. Members of an underprivileged minority in the United States, for them, "English often remains the foreign language of powerful and rich possibilities" (Perez-Torres 214).

Chicana American poet Carmen Tafolla recounts how English was an instrument of control in her school, where speaking Spanish was prohibited. The speaker in the poem "And When I Dream Dreams" states:

> ("You'll never get through high school
> speakin' Spanish," I was told)
> (nice of them, they thought, to not report me,
> breakin' state law, school law, speakin' dirty
>   [speaking spanish]
> and our tongues could not lump it
> and do what they were supposed to do.)
>
> (Five Poets, 223)

Speaking the native language in that environment is placed within a system of criminal activities. There are people who report on anyone who speaks Spanish; they admonish and forgive, thus setting up a hierarchy based on favors. The enforcement of English only aims to disinherit the child from her past by defaming it; it positions her in a subordinate relation with her peers and casts doubts on her potential.

In Chirtra Banarjee Divakaruni's poem "Yuba City School," an Indian Sikh woman whose son is not performing well in school describes her ordeal with the English language.

> Tomorrow in my blue skirt I will go
> to see the teacher, my tongue
> stiff and swollen
> in my unwilling mouth, my few
> English phrases. She will pluck them
> from me, nail shut my lips. My son
> will keep sitting in the last row
> among the red words that drink his voice.
>
> (Divakaruni 119)

The teacher's command of English and the speaker's lack of it allow the teacher full command of the situation. The teacher decides which of the speaker's words are appropriate for the situation and decides when to silence her. The son's continuing lack of command of the language places him at the bottom of the educational food chain "among the red words that drink his voice." For both the mother and the son, their weak command of English, and in turn their continued use of their native language, renders them passive. This association between lack of agency and the use of the native language is continuously reinforced in similar disempowering encounters with the English language.

While access to power is gained through English, it can create within the bilingual speaker a powerful resentment toward the adopted language. Speaking of "the man who owns the world," the Nuyorican poet Miguel Algarin proposes masochistic exorcism to rid him of the taint caused by unwilled adoption of the language of power:

> if all my talk is borrowed
> from his tongue then i want
> hot boiling water to wash
> out my mouth i want lye
> to soothe my soiled lips
> for the english that i
> speak betrays my need
> to be a self made power
>   (Mohr 120)

If the Puerto Rican begins to speak the "english" of the master then he is reaching for individual empowerment. Enrichment and empowerment are not repugnant in themselves. But the poet finds achieving them through the master language so revolting that only boiling water and lye can cleanse him. Of course, the severe and painful degree to which the poet is willing to punish himself situates the poet in a morally superior position. In declaring the extent of the punishment he is willing to inflict upon himself, he offers an unstated challenge to his audience. The powerful imaginary response to an imagined situation helps him gain a command of himself that he wishes to inspire within his community.

The fact that Algarin writes in English testifies to his belief in the availability of englishes outside the hegemony of the mainstream. Algarin's stance, and that of many Latino writers, resembles that of postcolonial writers in the English-speaking Caribbean and other former parts of the British empire where native languages disappeared. Ashcroft et al. have argued that postcolonial writers have indeed succeeded in transforming English to suit their surroundings. In fact, they argue it is no longer realistic to assume the existence of one standard English.

The development of other englishes is part of a larger strategy of resistance to colonization called the "creole continuum," which emerges out of two opposing impulses: abrogation and appropriation. Puerto Rican and Chicano/a poets, who are both immigrants and colonized subjects, reject the master language and attempt to purge themselves of it, but also appropriate aspects of it for their benefit. Dialects, with the dual techniques of abrogation and appropriation, created spaces for communication outside the master language. The idea here is "not a subversion of language alone, but of the entire system of cultural . . . metropolitan control" (48). Similarly, the postcolonial writer, by adopting the linguistic strategies of his region, can assert that the English language, employed in his/her hand, does not need a master code for its referentiality.

From a linguistic standpoint, all bilinguals speak an interlanguage even when they do not code-switch. For bilingual writers, the operative term for this creative process, in Chantal Zabus's view, is "relexification." Zabus argues that a bilingual does not write or think in her/his native language nor in their adopted one. Relexification "is characterized by the absence of an original. It therefore does not operate from the language of one text to the other but from one language to the other within the same text" (112). Because of the lack of an original and the individual way each bilingual writer goes about creating text, each "message event" can represent a wide variety of readings.

Relexification does not take place as a result of interference of the native language. Nor is relexification a nativization of an alien tongue or mere nonnative additions added to the alien tongue. A bilingual writer thinks from the standpoint of an "inter-language" and writes in a target language that constantly suggests another. Relexification, therefore, points to an author's innovations that do not reflect variations in any current oral usage either in the target language or in the writer's native language.

Zabus's notion of relexification rests on an assumption of the existence of individualized unverbalized lexicons upon which each bilingual's speech and writing are created. Other researchers have focused on code-switching. Among Latino poets, Spanish-English code-switching in poetry takes place as an expression of individuality but also reflects the way some Latinos actually speak. Poetry that adopts people's speech aims to legitimate it by demonstrating its expressive power. It empowers such speech and the people who speak it by creating a community of readers for it.

As in most bilingual speech practices the world over, code-switching "represents the creative use of both languages" (Dulay et al 118). Partly used to convey shared understanding and intimacy, code-switching can create speech-acts where words are displaced from their given meanings. The reassignment of signification, or language play, is employed poetically. A passage in a poem by Virgil combines English and Spanish to convey tone changes. The poem begins with a good deal of profanity and rhetorical posturing directed toward a certain macho character. At this point in the poem, the speaker wants to gain a different advantage, mainly to characterize herself as reasonable.

> whereas ordinarily
> out of common courtesy or stubbornness
> the ground I'd stand and argue principles—
> esta ve que no [not this time]
> porque esa clase de pendejadas [because that type of bullshit]
> mi tiempo fino no merece [doesn't merit my valuable time]
>
> (P-T, 299)

The English of lines 2 and 3 in this passage display a kind of official language where adversaries compete on rhetorical or legal grounds. The rest of this passage shifts to Spanish in which tough words are used again and where an informal sensibility is appealed to. The speaker displays a mastery of verbosity, qualities assigned here to English, but quickly insults the person addressed by returning to Spanish saying that he is not worthy of lofty rhetoric. The impact of the linguistic shift, both humorous and convincing, lends the passage a significance that is not possible using either one of the two languages.

Two lines later, the speaker demonstrates a different rhetorical gesture.

> I like to wear only shoes that fit
> me gusta andar comfortable [I like to go about comfortable]
>
> (240)

The poet uses the English "comfortable" instead of the Spanish "confortable." The play with the word "me" places these two lines in linguistic flux. As English readers, we assume that the first line is enjambed and the second follows to complete the phrase "fit me." "Me," however, is the subject for "I" in Spanish. The poet's resistance to present herself as an object in English in favor of being a subject in her native language resonates within this linguistic transfer as an ideologically significant gesture. The two sentences can appear as coming from two languages but also can appear to be a single English one. As English readers, our presumption of comprehension and our efforts to create a different meaning are quickly checked. Our mistaken assumption that the Spanish-speaking person has misused the English language turns out to be not only premature but conceivably embarrassing. Through strategic use of code-switching, the poet gains "authority" by demonstrating that she is in command of the situation and that we need her as a guide, suggesting that there are several reasons why we should stop and listen carefully to her, and in turn, to her people.

Latino poets, as they engage in issues specific to their community and as they address them through Spanish/English code-switching, still take into account the English-only speaker and reader, who may in fact be a member of their community. Latino American poetry, therefore, has to address an insider audience and an outsider one and speak for, and about, its community. This is an even more pressing issue for other bilingual poets. The written forms of their languages, their syntaxes, and etymological formulations, can be so different from English that they render a written bilingual practice extremely difficult. The insertion of the Arabic alphabet or Chinese characters may interrupt the reading experience, which in turn means losing the English-only speaker.

Nonetheless, non-Latino American bilingual poets from all sorts of ethnic and linguistic backgrounds have incorporated their native languages to some degree. Like African and Asian writers writing in English, they have utilized a number of techniques to convey particularities of their experiences (Kachru 128). These include the employment of certain rhetorical styles that cannot be identified as English. These include formal address, statements of endearment and deference, and phrases of direct address that are not used in English and are indicative of a different social order. Also, many American bilingual poets come from cultures that still have strong oral traditions, which they have tried to convey. They have also used non-Western, non-English literary forms. Additionally, non-native writers in English literally translate local metaphors, similes and proverbs instead of their English equivalents. These examples of figurative language become metonymic as they point to a larger system of values and explication not available in English. Additionally, "glossing," a borrowing technique where a foreign word or passage is used and a translation of it is provided immediately, is a common tool used by bilingual poets. In some cases, bilingual writers do not provide translations to force the reader into an active engagement with the culture from which these words emerge.

The aforementioned techniques empower the bilingual poet by allowing her to engage in finding the "exact" words for the conveyance of certain thoughts and feelings. One can think of a poet's bilinguality as simply an expanded vocabulary. Fresh metaphors and similes, new words, and turns of phrase demonstrate a writer's ability to reshape the language and also to imbue new meanings to certain situations. A literal translation, even of a foreign cliché, can provide a fresh metaphor in English.

Yugoslav-American poet Charles Simic, who immigrated to the United States as a teenager, presents an interesting example of the influence of bilingualism on his inception as a poet. His interest in American folklore (riddles, folktales, nursery rhymes, and proverbs) and his comparison between it and that of his Slavic heritage gave him a sense of the interchangeability of language (Simic 8). A story or a riddle can be changed or transformed if one were to change a single word. One of Simic's most anthologized poems, "My Neighbors the Hittites" draws a narrative scheme out of inverting a series of American proverbs. The result is one of the funniest and most original poems in contemporary American poetry. Another American poet, W. S. Di Piero, states that his family's intonations and speaking patterns in Italian provided him with interesting rhythms for his poetry (112). Putting English words to those rhythms allowed him to forge a voice for himself as a young poet and still sustains his writing.

Li-Young Lee's poem, "Persimmons," celebrates not only the bilingual poet's diction but also the bilingual's jumbling of his adopted language. The speaker of the poem recalls being smacked on the head by his grade school teacher for confusing the words "persimmon" and "precision." Attributing the mistake to his bilinguality, the poet takes full advantage of the incident. There is room, he asserts, for confusion as persimmons and precision are highly connected. He writes, "How to choose / persimmons. This is precision" (Lee, 19). He further elaborates, "it takes precision to choose a persimmon / and it takes precision to eat them (19).

A short stanza later in the poem, the poet lists other word confusions he faced as a child. These indicate opportunities for poems similar to this one. The following couplet describes his confusion between "fight" and "fright": "Fight was what I did when I was frightened / fright was what I felt when I was fighting (19). Lee displays a kind of "cunning," or coyness here that Gerald Stern discusses in the introduction to the volume *Rose* from which this poem comes. Listing these words, the poet boasts of his technique. My life is full of such confusions, and I can write a poem of each one of them, he seems to say. That these two lines form a couplet, rhymed and metrically perfect, boldly demonstrates his prowess.

Lee's poem demonstrates that a celebration of one's ethnic culture in the United States cannot occur without addressing how that culture relates to the mainstream. This is more true in the case of cultures that do not come from European-Christian origins. The language issue plays an informative role here in voicing criticisms of the United States as a nation and as a culture. Marilyn Chin's poem, "Barbarian Suite," takes its title from a term historically used by the Chinese to describe basically all foreigners, all those outside the middle kingdom. A Chinese-American poet born in Hong Kong, Chin begins the poem with a pun on an American folk song.

> My loss is your loss, a dialect here, a memory there—
> if my left hand is dying will my right hand cut it off?
> We shall all be vestigial organs, the gift of democracy.
> The pale faces, the wan conformity,
> the price we pay for comfort is our mother tongue.
> (Chin, 48)

Beginning with "my loss is your loss," Chin reinvisions America not as a land of prosperity but as a site of sacrifice and surrender. The immigrant's native language, the "dialect" mentioned in the poem, is the first of these losses. Loss of memories follows. In this social order, the immigrant's assimilation, like a virgin's chastity, is needed to maintain the larger culture's purity. But such sacrifices do not reward; rather, they lead to a process of disowning, with the loss of the native language at its center.

The passage that follows explores further the immigrants' political inertia, particularly in relation with their native land.

> China is an ocean away, our grandmother beaconing
> with too many children, too many mouths to feed.
> We can no longer dress her and improve her accent.
> We can no longer toil in her restaurant "Double
>   Happiness," oiling woks, peeling shrimp.

> She is the bridge—and we've broken her back with our weight.
> We study Western philosophy and explore our raison d'etre.
> All is well in the suburbs when we are in love with poetry.
>
> (48)

The "we" in the poem, immigrant Chinese like the poet herself, are weary of trying to improve their native land's situation. The options are limited to trying to contain her limitations (improve her accent), and toiling in her restaurant. These criticisms of Chinese-America—the children's anxiety over their parents' accents and the limitations of the parents' intellectual pursuits—also provide a critique of the larger culture with its stigmatization of people with accents and of the professional pigeonholing that occurs in the world of business and employment. The kind of comfort the first immigrants traded their native languages for metamorphosizes among their offspring into activities such as exploring "Western philosophy and . . . our raison d'etre." These developments, however lofty, represent a transformation from a dynamic communal sense to seclusion and apathy. The poem suggests that the loss of the native language initiates this fall into indifference.

Like Marilyn Chin, Lisel Mueller, winner of the 1997 Pulitzer Prize in poetry, takes her cue from a famous American phrase to title one of her poems. In the first section of "Your Tired, Your Poor," Mueller, who was born in Germany and immigrated to the United States as a young adult, portrays the emigrants' native languages and their memories as possessions they have to smuggle behind their eyes and under their tongues. As the stanza progresses, the immigrant's native language transforms from a hidden aspect to "a yellow star." The stanza gains it rhetorical momentum through a layering of metaphors that seem contradictory at times. But there is no mistaking the burden of the native language on the immigrant.

When the immigrant's reluctant assimilation occurs, it seems at times sudden and uncontrollable:

> you find yourself humming the music
> you stuffed your ears against
> you dream in rhyme in a language
> you never wanted to understand
>
> (Mueller 163)

The music that has to be fought off still compels its listeners to hum it. The language that one never wanted to understand takes over one's subconscious. Later in the stanza, the voices from home are "bent by the ocean," and other objects associated with home begin to seem strange. As a compensation, these formerly familiar places begin to offer their own delights, and ironically, one finds pleasure in viewing them. As opposed to patriotism and acceptance of a national framework we encounter ambivalence, a kind of nostalgia, a state of existential calm steeped in irony. In the new country, in a new language, one is not quite empowered with living in the present; in fact, one's only sense of living in the present occurs through realizing that the past is irretrievably gone.

Besides making the full realization of the present impossible, the existence of an earlier language and an earlier life causes other experiences of discontent and disconnection. In his poem "In Language," Filipino-born poet, Eugene Gloria, describes an encounter with a lover with whom he remains in a limited kind of intimacy because of the language difference.

> After we make love I teach you
> words I'm slowly forgetting . . .
>
>   I teach you, to remind
> Myself . . .
>   (Gloria 143)

The passing on of the language is meant to enhance the speaker's memory. These fading words, the poet implies, need to be remembered by more than one person.

He needs his lover to help reach a part of him that he can only approach indirectly now. He needs an outsider's evocation of things familiar to him. But the lover fails to learn. Addressing her, the poet says

> you say
> hair instead of river; you say breasts,
> instead of hands, you say
> cock and cunt
> instead of moon, sea, and stars
>   (143)

Her vocabulary remains fixated on the sexual encounter and sexual organs while the poet attempts to expand their shared experience to things outside of themselves. The poem ends with that note of frustration. As he aims to take both of them to rivers, moon, sea, and stars—toward transcendence—the beloved holds the poet to the body of breasts, cock and cunt.

The poetry of bilinguals in America, and to some extent all minority literatures, vacillates between the desire to address the mainstream and to ignore the center in order to feel that its experience is the center of all existence. The double consciousness that Du Bois eloquently attributes to African-Americans in fact lives within all who feel between two places, two languages. The twentieth century, horrible as it has been, has also been a revolutionary time as far as sounding the voices of the dispossessed. In James Fennimore Cooper's novels of the American colonial era, the natives of the land speak, but only through an interpreter who has mastered their language. And not a single word of the natives' languages appears. In the soldiers tents' of the Revolutionary War and the American Civil War, not only were there a myriad of English accents spoken but a heap of languages as well. Walt Whitman contained multitudes but detested the foreign born. Little remains now of the various works that were written in other languages here in the United States. The U.S. canon does not contain a work of literature that was not written in English.

Such silencing could not go on forever. The linguistic mix we encounter in the immigrants' poetry, the accents, and the borrowings have always been part of the American daily experience. The way we work now and live around the world, with so much mobility and flux, has made the experience of the immigrant representative of much of what we go through in both the tangible and the metaphysical sense. The bilingual poetry written now in the United States rejuvenates our English, our main medium of exchange, bringing the world to us and allowing us to communicate better with the world. In poetry, as it is practiced today in the United States, America comes closest to its ideals. The freedom of expression is wider in American poetry than it is anywhere else in any legal or poetic tradition. For now, and following the best of America's legacies, what little each of us knows is valuable and empowering, and what we do not know about each other forms the frontier we now must explore. Poetry, as always, is already a few steps ahead of us in the endeavor.

Works Cited

Chin, Marilyn. *The Phoenix Gone, The Terrace Empty*. New York: W. W. Norton, 1994.

Daydi-Tolson, Santiago. *Five Poets from Aztlan*. Binghamton, NY: Bilingual Press, 1985.

Di Piero, W. S. "Gots Is What You Got," *Best American Essays, 1995* (Jamaica Kincaid, ed.). New York, Vantage, 1995.

Divakaruni, Chirtra Banarjee. "Yuba City School" in *Open Boat, An Anthology of Asian American Poetry*, Hongo, Garret, ed. New York: Anchor Books, 1992.

Dulay, Heidi; Burt, Marina; Krashen, Stephen. *Language* 2. New York: Oxford University, 1982.

Gloria, Eugene. "In Language," *Open Boat, An Anthology of Asian American Poetry*, Hongo, Garret, ed. New York: Anchor Books, 1992, 43–44.

Kachru, Braj. *The Alchemy of English*, Urbana: University of Illinois Press, 1990.

Lee, Li-Young. *Rose*. Brockport, NY: Boa Editions, 1986.

Mohr, Eugene V. *The Nuyorican Experience: Literature of the Puerto Rican Minority*. Greenwood Press. Westport, CT: 1982.

Mueller, Lisel. *Alive Together: New and Selected Poems*. Baton Rouge: Louisiana State University, 1996.

Perez-Torres, Rafael, *Movements in Chicano/a Poetry: Against Myths, Against Margins*. Cambridge University. New York: 1995.

Simic, Charles. *The Uncertain Certainty*, Ann Arbor: University of Michigan Press, 1985.

Zabus, Chantal. *The African Palimpsest: Indegenization of Language in the West African Europhone Novel*, Cross Cultures 4, Amsterdam and Atlanta: Rodopi, 1991.

Ethnic American Writing and the Challenge of Tradition

Though the title of this talk refers to writing, I'm thinking mainly about poetry. What difference does it make to focus on poetry as opposed to another genre? That has something to do with what critic John Reilly called "the raw material" of literature, or the easy access to the "ethnic" element in an ethnic literary work. The other reason has to do with poetry as a genre, when looking at a poem, we note that several artistic aspects rear their heads, to the point that one cannot talk about a poetic text without addressing—or wanting to address—its formal elements. If a poem does not have enough poetry in it to be a poem, why is it poetry then? And if it is poem, what are the poetic elements doing to carry the content, if indeed the two can be separated? Given that poetry pronounces its artistry, there is perhaps a sense whereby one cannot easily parse the poetry into ethnic quarters.

The same applies to theatre. There is so much involved in the craft of writing and performing it that the form dominates the ethnic label. Perhaps for that reason, I never quite think of August Wilson as part of African American theatre. Or even *A Raisin in the Sun*, the famous play by Lorraine Hansberry. I know that both are African American playwrights, and their works are performed by African American actors, but, in my mind, they are not only part of African American theatre.

The same can be said about jazz, where African American artists may still be the majority, but is the art form still African American per se? It seems to me that at this point jazz is jazz, there is no black jazz versus white jazz, nor Polish versus Swedish jazz. Jazz is just jazz.

Is poetry, poetry then, or is it ethnic still? I'll not answer this question just yet, or maybe never. As to whether there's such a thing as African American poetry? Yes, there is. But is it ethnic poetry in the sense of it being a literature set aside, written and read by members of a given community. Certainly not. In fact, given that many African poets are recognized by the poetry establishment and academia, it is hard to think of African American poetry as having a realm of its own separate from American poetry. I can't historically account for when that shift happened, but let's say that there's been a shift away from the ethnic, even as the poetry has become mainstream.

It seems to me that ethnic is a temporary label, given to a group by others or by its members, as they emerge or coalesce, and as they push for recognition. But is it something they want to stick to, at the exclusion of every other possibility? Probably not. Taking up an ethnic American identity could be a step, a big step, on the route to assimilation, as anthropologist Andrew Shryock has argued. However, there is the fact of racism, which makes ethnic identity a place of affirmation and a sort of safe house during times of crisis. No ethnic writer who has identified as such wishes not to be ethnic, but perhaps no writer wants to write only ethnic literature.

1.

And by the way what is ethnic literature? The aforementioned critic John M. Reilly, back in 1978 in one of the early issues of *MELUS*, the journal of the Society for the Study of the Multi-Ethnic Literature of the United States, defined ethnic literature as "a literature like any other except that it has ethnic references"[1] (2). Good enough! So what's the problem? The problem is what happens to the literariness of ethnic literature. The problem is that oftentimes ethnic literature is not read as literature at all. People who are less acquainted with ethnic literature may be drawn to "the verisimilitude of the narration so completely that they take the literature as an equivalence of life," whereby the artistic devices are "presumed references of objective reality" (2). As such, ethnic literature becomes equated with a sort of anthropology, rather than a form of art. Even "expert readers . . acting upon 'ethnic'" as the active ingredient often "seek to recover the *raw material*[2] of the author's story from the creative deformation it has undergone in becoming plot, characterization, and style" (2).

Reading ethnic literature this way, readers may perceive the ethnic writer as someone who does not work hard, who's simply telling his life story, who's not imaginative or inventive. And there are ample examples of this misperception. In Nam Le's meta-fictional story "Love and Honour and Pity and Pride and Compassion and Sacrifice," the protagonist (ironically and metafictionally named Nam Le) is told by his classmates "ethnic lit" makes them sick, as "it's full of descriptions of exotic food," or that the language might be "sparse because the author . . . didn't have the vocab."[3] Another friend says, ethnic literature is "a license to bore."[4]

"Ethnic" literature when seen as merely content, deprives it of the status of art and deems it as propaganda for temporal causes, not art made to endure. When it's seen as something people engage in as a matter of politics it loses its association with the imagination and the enduring human tensions, which are not ethnic. The implication here is such "universal," "human" concerns are better dealt with in regular vanilla literature.

Yet, despite these problematic aspects, ethnic literature has its allure. The character Nam in Nam Le's story is told to capitalize on his ethnic background. His instructor tells him, "Ethnic literature is hot. And important too" (Le 9). He is told also to exploit the Vietnam material, for exploitation is what one does to strange material.

The success, or hotness, of "ethnic literature" has had its negative effects on the writer in other ways. Convinced of his "authenticity," the ethnic writer may begin to trade in raw materials and to forsake artistry. His community may be so harassed that he has no time or inclination to write "literary" literature. The Arab/Muslim American community is a case in point—a community that has crisis in its very basis. Here, issues of survival must be dealt with and addressed now. But responses to these events, in the literary sense, may be very limited, however effective they may be politically.

Compelled by authentic need, a sense of identity borne in crisis, a young Arab/Muslim American can begin a literary endeavor with a set of basic themes. First, there's the sense of being outside the fold. A poet may write, "I landed in America / Might as well say the moon." A sense of loss and a longing for a better more wholesome world also may permeate this poetry. Dealing with American consumer products, a character in an Arab American text will favor "Shaka's soap from Nablus . . . / not Ivory, Dove, or Dial (Hasan)."[5] Such alienation and displacement bring about a feeling of lack, or even self-loathing. Thus monstrified by establishment culture, one speaker in an Arab American poem imagines that he was assembled by a taxidermist who, "has done a wonderful job . . . / So wonderful, my mouth could speak (Mekouar)."[6] An encounter with authority, a racist boss or co-worker, or the police . . . introduces a kind of Manichean reductionism as in the following lines:

> We—since our infancy—sit at the trailhead of two paths:
> one paved in Coke cans,
> the other as mysterious as camel humps in moonlight.
> And a struggle ensues,
> between the Rababa and Rock n' Roll...[7]

Positioning herself or himself as such, a young Arab American writer cannot go very far in the ghetto of raw material literature where the theme is ready-made and ripe for class discussion.

Another aspect of ghettoized literature, in addition to the focus on raw material, is the sense of protectiveness of one's group that girds the work. While editing *Post Gibran: An Anthology of Arab American Writing* and having read quite a few good submissions for it, I realized that only a few could be considered daring or risky. A handful broke taboos or challenged conceptions shared by the Arab American community. Perhaps we, Arab American writers, avoid controversy because we fear the very likely possibility that that information be used against us, thus possibly reinforcing the stereotypes that have been imposed upon us. As it stands now, writing in survival mode persists as a starting point. A literature that speaks for a community while protecting it ceases to be engaged in a conversation with literary models or any particular tradition and as such gives up the ability to renew itself. The attractiveness of raw materials writing along with protectiveness combine to deter artistry and complexity, and in that sense, fulfill some of the stereotypes of ethnic literature.

2.

An ambitious ethnic writer, who is in fact informed by literary history and wants to take on a revolutionary stance toward the art form, not just a revolutionary political stance, may want to join the avant-garde as it promises a larger transformation. The avant-garde insists on restructuring "society as a whole and all its institutions... Everyday life, art and the political life; all must be torn down and a new society, a new way of living which integrates all of these aspects in one, must be constructed from the ground" (Bisberg and Rasmussen).[8] Since mainstream art does not aspire to change society, it is "not just useless but actually harmful in its reproduction of the existing structures of power and society" (Ibid.). Conceptually, the avant-garde provides opportunities for shedding inhibitions, direct confrontation, trusting intuition, and total transformation of society and consciousness, and in that sense, is immensely appealing to a member of a beleaguered minority. That's all well and good. But historically, the avant-garde, whether it's futurism in Europe in the early decades of the twentieth century, or even the benign Beats in the United States, has not been a hospitable place for minorities or for women for that matter.

In a recent essay, the critically acclaimed experimental Korean American poet Cathy Park Hong gives a powerful testimony to the continuing intolerance of the literary avant-garde. In "Delusions of Whiteness in the Avant-Garde (Hong)."[9] Hong pulls no punches declaring that "to encounter the history of avant-garde poetry is to encounter a racist tradition." Hong takes on the notion of "post-identity," which is a basic tenet in the American avant-garde, a tenet that dismisses the struggles and concerns of writers of color. Writers cannot afford "the luxurious opinion that anyone can be 'post-identity' and can casually slip in and out of identities like a video game avatar" (Hong). She dismisses the avant-garde's "specious belief that renouncing subject and voice is antiauthoritarian, when in fact such wholesale pronouncements are clueless that the disenfranchised need such bourgeois niceties like voice to alter conditions forged in history." She considers this assumption a delusion that denies writers of color the opportunity to resist the authoritarian practices in American society on issues that affect them. She denounces the fact that race or racial politics have no place in avant-garde circles. As in Nam Le's short story, addressing racism (identity politics) in the current avant-garde esthetic of post-identity denies an ethnic writer any claim on innovation. Hong asserts that it's impossible to be post-racial or post-identity and dismiss poetics when one is always read as a poet of color, in other words a poet of limited concerns.

Hong also finds it troubling that much of the current avant-garde's so-called innovations are in fact borrowed from poets of color: She writes,

> If we are to acknowledge that there are formal choices that define avant-garde poetry such as polyvocality, hybridity, collage, stream-of-conscious writing, and improvisation, these techniques were not only used but were actually first inaugurated by writers of African and Asoan descent such as Jean Toomer, Aimé Césaire, Leopold Senghor, and Theresa Hak Kyung Cha . . . Many of these poets' reputations have long been battened under the banner of ethnic studies but are rarely regarded as core figures in experimental poetry.

One can add many names to the list Hong presents here. I should say that this discussion of exclusion from the realm of experimentation is one that I've had with several Arab American poets, who also feel that despite their innovativeness, they are repeatedly denied the term experimental, and are only invited to speak about the political or other thematic aspects of their work, the raw materials, not their formal inventions.

So with the ethnic ghetto not a happy place, the main market place a dubious location, and the avant-garde loft also an unwelcoming abode, it's no wonder we have many young poets who naturally begin with the themes outlined earlier and, after exhausting them, have nothing to say and give up writing all together.

Hong and I converge at this point. She asks, "So what is a poet of color to do?" and I wrote down at the beginning of these thoughts, "Where is a poet of color to go?" It's also where we separate.

Beginning a crescendo-like incantation, Hong declares the spirit of experimentation remains vital in the work of the poets of color. The new ethnic arts cross genres and break down all barriers between artistic disciplines.

> The voices have returned, minstrelized, digitalized, theatricalized artifice, speaking in a mélange of offshoots . . . The form is code-switching: code-switching between languages, between Englishes, between genres, between races, between bodies. New ethnic American artists are "building a new, dissonant futurism, treating poetry as rank growth as it punctures the dying medium of print via performance, video, or audio recordings."

The new poets are making sure that "poetry can continue to be a site of agitation, where the audience is . . . provoked into participatory response." "But will these poets ever be accepted as the new avant-garde?" asks Hong at the conclusion of her essay. Briefly, the answer is "No! "Fuck the avant-garde. We must hew our own path," she concludes.

3.

While I agree with Hong's call to fuck the avant-garde, I say the challenge for ethnic poets lies also in their ability to investigate their literary heritages. But let me first be very clear that we are doomed if we study our various cultural heritages to repeat what these historical epochs practiced. As Ezra Pound noted in his embrace of his literary ancestors, we read the ancients to find out "what has been done, once and for all, better than it can ever be done again, and to find out what remains for us to do."[10] We do indeed feel the same emotions as our ancestors, but "we come on these feelings differently, through different nuances, by different intellectual gradations." In terms of form, parroting one's predecessors damages our relations to older texts, obscuring their impression on our memory because the new that repeats the old is said "with less skill and less conviction." Those of us who read classical Arabic poetry get that queasy feeling when we hear a new poet sounding like the old. We feel it like an act of desecration, a kind of imitation that menaces us with its vacuousness.

As I propose a relationship with tradition, I want to acknowledge that such a relationship is also confrontational. We cannot help but confront the old if we are to take it seriously. One turns to a tradition because it has a set of ideas to which he or she is invariably attached and because it allows the new writer to negotiate his or her current experiences through them. We turn to the old to help imagine other possible facets in our contemporary life.

I take this position regarding tradition (and history) because I am not deceived by the present moment and its claims on progress. I concur with the Syrian/Lebanese poet Adonis, who stated that "the essence of progress is . . . qualitative not quantitative" (Adonis, 96).[11] He adds that "The Westerner who lives surrounded by computers and exposed to the latest space travel is not necessarily more advanced, or more free," (96) by virtue of his technological advances. Furthermore, let me cite the Brazilian scholar Oswald de Andrade who explained his interest in studying the indigenous peoples of the Amazon saying, "The Indian had no police, no repression, no nervous disorders, no shame at being nude, no class struggle, no slavery" (quoted in Stam).[12] Certainly, I'm not inviting you or myself to take up peasantry or to live like as an aboriginal of the Amazon, if only not to disgrace such authenticity with our clumsiness. Yet, all epochs of high human achievement wherever they occur are worthy of our attention if we are to address the dominant paradigms that have extenuated class divisions, institutionalized poverty and exploited racial differences. And in the literary sense, the past is worthy of our attention as a source of allusion and shared myths, as a record of how we differed from our present selves. Without that awareness we will not have the courage real change requires.

But let me return to the Arab American writer in particular. Exploring tradition may offer also a rich source of formal innovation. I am convinced that formal innovations by necessity result in innovations in tone and content. It would make a difference, therefore, for the Arab American poet to study the Qassida tradition and its complicated and utterly fascinating epic/lyric structure. The sa'aluk poets are worthy challengers for the claim of rebelliousness given to Baudelaire and Villon. It would be energizing for the Arab American writer to study Abu Nawwas, an openly gay tenth century poet who recited his poems in the caliph's court in Baghdad, a feat we have yet to see repeat itself anywhere. Ibn Khaldun's chapter on poetry in the *Muqadimma* provides a fascinating discourse on poetics when read alongside Aristotle's *Poetics*. Rabi'a al-'Adawiya's twining of erotic and spiritual love is still relevant to our spirit-body crisis. The young Arab American poet, studying these sources with an understanding of current sociopolitical and spiritual crises, versed as she is in American rhythms and language, may in fact be able to begin developing a nuanced vision or critique relevant to us all. By that, I don't mean that the ethnic writer has to solve all his society's problems, but he is aware that others exist alongside him.

4.

And if I am to take a guess, what an Arab American needs mostly is a sense of freedom and affirmation, a reading experience that will encourage her right not only to gain the full freedom she needs, but also the right to explore the whole world and to see it anew. Thus, an ethnic/multicultural text succeeds, I believe, when alluding to its source traditions to redefine our current surroundings cosmologically, ontologically, and epistemologically. In other words, such texts can't be reduced to raw material literature. Some ethnic American poets have succeeded in doing so. Poet Arthur Sze has carved a unique place for himself in American poetry by bringing to the landscape of the American West the Zen and Taoist strains that have long influenced the poetic tradition of his Chinese ancestors. Like the ancient poet Wang Wei in his walking travels and their engrossment with/in landscape, Sze offers us the American West with a unique quiescence. The poet seems to disappear in his full merging with nature; he is one among many like a figure in a painting. The poem serves as a mirror in which nature and existence are reflected, and equally, nature is a mirror in which the poet, among other things, is reflected. Listen with me to these lines:

> "Eat," a man from Afghanistan said
> and pointed to old rotting apples in the opened car trunk.
> I see a line of men dancing a cloud dance;
> two women dance intricate lightning steps
> at either end. My mistakes and failures
> pulse in me even as moments of joy,
> but I want the bright moments to resonate out
> like a gamelan gong. I want to make
> the intricate tessellated moments of our lives
> a floor of jade, obsidian, turquoise, ebony, lapis. (Sze, 124)[13]

Different geographies are brought together here: A man from Afghanistan, native Americans performing a ritual dance, and Chinese artifacts. In this poem about the creation of art, the poet wishing to make some moments of his life endure chooses two Chinese symbols, the gamelan gong, and the materials of Chinese jewelry and antiques. In many ways, this poem encapsulates what the late Stuart Hall means about identity as a place to speak from. Sze is contemplating two sides of America, the new immigrant to the land and its natives, and weaves them together, positioning himself as an artisan rendering the scene. Without this allusion to tradition, Sze would not have had a unique speaking position. His tradition, his sense of historical entitlement to Chinese artistry, gives him his voice here, and a unique one at that, to address the world.

Chinese tradition also plays an important role in Li-Young Lee's work. In the poems in his volume *Rose*, Lee establishes, in a very subtle manner, new articulations to the sense of belonging and to our notions of place in America. The scene of visiting the father's grave recurs in several poems in the volume, and the practice serves as an important locational ritual for the family in the midst of exile. Recognizing his ancestral veneration of the dead, the speaker in the "Rain Diary" states:

> I asked once, Where are we going?
> My question could have been, In what country
> will your pillow finally come to rest . . .
> As a boy I lay quietly beside him while he napped.
> I was practicing to lie down
> by his grave . . . (Lee, 60)[14]

The wanderings of exile end at the father's burial place. The speaker suggests that the place we call home is the place we bury our ancestors as that is the moment when one actually puts down roots. The image of the boy sleeping beside his father recurs in another poem in which the poet, now an adult, falls asleep near his father's grave with his own son lying beside him. In addition to being an occasion to gather the members of the family, visiting the father's grave serves as an important ontological reconceptualization of time dissolving the binary tension between past and future, and, in doing so, expanding our sense of the present moment. In the midst of exile, home is not the place our children are born or where our future plans are plotted but where we have a past. Filled with the poet's "long stemmed grief," these moments also ring with a redemptive note that sounds the onset of the poet's sense of rootedness.

For another example of how ethnic American poets have incorporated their traditions to provide radical visions, I would like to turn to Leslie Marmon Silko's poem, "Long Time Ago," from her remarkable novel *Ceremony*. The poem is a historical interpretation of American history presented as legend in the tradition of Silko's Laguna Pueblo ancestors. As a ruse, the poem begins with a witchery contest when:

> there were no white people in this world
> there was nothing European . . .
> The world was already complete . . .
> There was everything
> including witchery (Silko, 122)[5]

Silko is enough of a genuine artist not to set the world of her ancestors as some innocent haven. The witches are engaged in showing each other up, the more expert among them lifting "the lids /of their big cooking pots . . . / dead babies simmering in blood/circles of skull cut away/all the brains sucked out." They are experts in evil arts and willing to outdo each other. Evil, Silko is willing to admit, did exist among her peoples, this being a conference that included witches from Navajo, Hopi, Zuni, Sioux, and Eskimo lineage. But they were yet to be outdone. One witch "who hadn't shown off charms or powers" revealed to them the most devastating trick of all: the arrival of European invaders to America. These invaders:

> When they look
>   they see only objects.
> The world is a dead thing for them
>   the trees and rivers are not alive

> the mountains and stones are not alive.
> The deer and bear are objects
> They see no life . . .
> They will kill the things they fear
> all the animals
> the people will starve.
> They will poison the water
> they will spin the water away
> and there will be drought
> the people will starve . . . (Silko, 122)[16]

The witch's devastating vision continues incorporating within it strife among the invaders, a subtle allusion to the European and American wars that occurred on this continent. The other witches readily acknowledge the witch as winner but immediately ask that she take back her witchery. "We are doing okay without it / we can get along without that kind of thing," they tell her. But she declares that "It's already turned loose / It's already coming."

As if to emphasize the collective unconscious depth of her vision, Silko here incorporates within the poem the biblical tale of Moses and the magicians, as well as the horror outlined in the Book of Revelations. Horrified as we may feel after reading this poem, we have a deeper understanding of our nation's legacy. The poem is not only a Native American poem, it is a brilliant and devastating American poem that derives its richness from a long-held tradition and that has tuned its incisive eyes on our history. And for sheer ambition let me point to Jay Wright's remarkable book-length poem, *The Double Invention of Komo*. In his informative afterword to the book, Wright writes:

> The Double Invention of Komo seeks to redeem and to discover social, historical, cultural, intellectual, and emotional dimensions now obscured in the African and Afro-American worlds and to make these dimensions available for creative use in the necessary transformation of an enhanced world of intransigent act. (Wright, xi)[17]

I can't think of a better description of the multicultural vision I hope I've articulated from the point of an Arab American writer. Impossible to paraphrase and difficult to excerpt without much contextualization, *The Double Invention of Komo* begins with the Bambara initiation ritual as a point of departure to view history. Implicit in the poem is the juxtaposition between the ambitions of the initiation rites and the social circumstances of a historical renaissance. Komo's inner journey toward initiation is juxtaposed throughout the poem with passages spoken by various European artists and authors speaking from London, Paris, Venice, Rome, Florence, and other cradles of Euro-American civilization. Part of the poem's working assumptions is the Bambara notion that society "is a living, articulated body, where all parts have complementary roles in constant relation." The initiate's effort to negotiate the signs of ritual rites toward self-invention is complimented by a chorus of artists who have initiated themselves into alternate, and sometimes controversial, views of the world. All have to contend with the ideal set by the Bambara tradition. For the Komo and the European characters, knowledge of history and cosmology coalesce toward an urgent need for a vision of the future, toward healing the body of society.

5.

A conceptually complex poem written in a demanding, yet highly lyrical, language, Wright's book is a deeply personal one. The poet's invention of the initiate, and the initiate's utterance of the poem, serve to address "the world to which the poem speaks," in other words to address Jay Wright's world. The doubleness referred to in the poem's title also suggests Wright's double inheritance, an African history that he raises to the surface and the history of Western civilization that he must know in order to address his predicament as the descendent of African slaves captured to build European hegemony. Wright's attempt to redeem "social, historical, cultural, intellectual, and emotional dimensions now obscured in the African and Afro-American worlds" does not constitute a nationalist or racialist project solely for the purpose of ethnic pride, or aim to locate an "authentic" dogma to replace a borrowed or imposed one. The multiplicity of voices that traverse time and place in the poem suggests inclusion rather than exclusion. He also points to the dialogue that must take place "in the necessary transformation of an enhanced world of intransigent act."

If the latter two texts discussed above share one quality that makes them successful, it is their reinvention of ritual in order to address the challenges of our present world. This approach has been with us for a long time, as far as the American experience is concerned. In 1925, the Afro-Latino American historian and author, Arturo Schomburg, wrote "The American Negro must *remake* his past in order to make his future" (Schomburg 231).[18] I would change Schomburg's "his" to "our." To remake one's past, is to make *our* future. In a world of environmental racism; demonization of all forms of otherness; unnecessary and unjust wars; . . . and the ceaseless oppression of women, children, and people of color across the globe, I believe that exploring the past, both history and literary inheritance, can widen the open invitation to change course and the ability to rename the destination. The world needs our thinking and rethinking, the old stories artfully retold and the stories never heard.

Notes

1. Reilly, John M. "Criticism of Ethnic Literature." *MELUS*, vol. 5, no. 1, (Spring 1978), pp. 2–13.
2. Italics mine.
3. Le, Nam. "Love and Honour and Pity and Pride and Compassion and Sacrifice," http://www.all-story.com/issues.cgi?action=show_story&story_id=305
4. Le, Nam. "Love and Honour and Pity and Pride and Compassion and Sacrifice," http://www.all-story.com/issues.cgi?action=show_story&story_id=305
5. Hasan, Aida. "Everything." *Mizna*. http:/www.mizna.org/vol2issue2/everthing.html
6. Mekouar, Hassan. *Mizna*. http:/www.mizna.org/vol2issue2/recipe.html
7. Riad, Shareef. "Xenogenesis," http://www.mizna.org/vol2issue1/Xenogenesis.html
8. Bisberg, Nanna Katrine and Rasmussen, Jan Nejdl. "The Manifesto: Text and Praxis." http://www.avantgardenet.eu/HAC/student/manifesto.pdf
9. http://www.lanaturnerjournal.com/print-issue-7-contents/delusions-of-whiteness-in-the-avant-garde
10. http://www.english.illinois.edu/maps/poets/m_r/pound/retrospect.htm
11. Adonis. *An Introduction to Arab Poetics*, translated by Catherine Cobham. London: Saqi Book, 1990.
12. Stam, Robert. *Reflexivity in Film and Literature: From Don Quixote to Jean-Luc Godard*. New York: Columbia University Press, 1992.
13. Sze, Arthur. *The Red Shifting Web: New & Selected Poems*. Port Townsend, WA: Copper Canyon Press, 2013.
14. Lee, Li-Young. *Rose*. Rochester, NY: BOA Editions, 1986.
15. Silko, Leslie Marmon. *Ceremony*. New York: Penguin Books, 1977.
16. Ibid.
17. Wright, Jay. *The Double Invention of Komo*. Austin, TX: University of Texas Press, 1980.
18. Schomburg, Arthur. "The Negro Digs Up His Past." In *Harlem, Mecca of the New Nesto*, A. Locke, editor. New York: Black Classic Press, 1925.

Writing Islam in Contemporary American Poetry
On Mohja Kahf, Daniel Moore and Agha Shahid Ali

It's become quite apparent that a growing body of Muslim literature written in European languages is emerging in France, Germany, Scandinavia, the Netherlands, Britain, the United States, and even Italy. The authors of this body of literature are outside two folds: Western literature per se and the literatures of their Muslim societies of origin. How do Muslim authors, specifically poets, fashion a voice when they are writing mostly to outsiders? What subject matter will they treat and in what manner? This essay explores these questions by examining how writing Islam is exercised differently by three American Muslim poets, Mohja Kahf, Daniel Moore and the late Agha Shahid Ali.

1.

In *E-Mails from Scheherazad* (2003), the poems of Mohja Kahf are primarily concerned with demystifying Muslim lives and practices in the United States and in altering misconceptions about Muslim women. These aims fall in line with Kahf's scholarly work, specifically her book *Western Representations of the Muslim Woman: From Termagant to Odalisque* (1999) and her fiction, most recently the novel *Girl in a Tangerine Scarf* (2006). Aiming to educate non-Muslim audiences and to empower fellow Muslim women, Kahf's poems sometimes home in on one segment of her potential readers. In the "Hijab Scene" poems we have two cases of comparative estrangement: a Muslim woman wearing a hijab is confronted by a pierced, blue-haired punk teenager and a heavily made-up, skimpily dressed woman. Who is weirder, who is more conformist, the poems ask. If the American woman is acquiescing to a condescending form of male taste and the punk teenager is conforming to a fad, why is the hijab wearing woman not their equal, and why is she not equally tolerated? The poet anticipates the answer her generally tolerant poetry reading audience will give her, which is, yes, by all means, the hijab-clad woman is their equal and should be equally tolerated.

In the poem "My Babysitter Wears a Face Veil," Kahf expects resistance and thus needs a larger, more sympathetic portrayal of Salwa, the khimar/burqa-wearing subject of her poem. Kahf renders the babysitter's veil as part of nature, and a magnificent part at that, since it shows her eyes "like the dark parts of the Himalayan mountains peeking" (32). Though startled drivers are watching Salwa, she has a sense of humor that allows her to be sympathetic toward the gawkers past whom she barrels in her four-by-four. The poem ends with an image of Salwa waiting at a traffic light, where the music she and another woman driver favor is drowned out by an ad for a monster truck show blaring from a male trucker's stereo. Having set the scene for solidarity between Muslim and non-Muslim women, the poet then wonders why people do not "see behind the blind spot for an instant" (33). When the light changes, the poem affirms that Salwa is like everyone else, a hardworking American who is improving her English and working on her GED. She just happens to wear a face veil, that's all.

Kahf presents us with situations that are familiar in our era of diversity discourse, where strangers are confronted with their difference and where it is the poet's job to defend them. This defense of individual rights and the right to worship and believe fits well into the role of the poet in general as a defender of individual choice. On the other hand, I cannot think of a contemporary, non fundamentalist poet in the Muslim world who would write such an adoring portrait of a woman wearing a face veil. This attire is considered extreme and threatening among the vast majority of the literati in the Muslim world. It is also attire imposed on Muslim populations by the most extreme Islamist groups and governments. But Kahf is not in conversation with her fellow Muslims in the Muslim world. As she addresses a largely Western audience, she presents portraits of persecuted Muslims and, through them, challenges the contemporary diversity discourse to make room for them. In the poem "My Body Is Not Your Battle Ground," Kahf, who is one of a generation of feminist and Muslim-identified writers, critiques both Western and Muslim patriarchies. She demands that imperialist Westerners and their moral equivalents, the antiimperialist Muslim chauvinists, cease using the Muslim female body as pretense for political violence, which has nothing to do with liberating or protecting women. Kahf pursues this idea further by expressing an assertive version of female desire, which would displease both Muslim extremists and Westerners whose sympathy or antipathy to Islam relies on stereotypical views of Muslim women as docile and repressed. Here's a poem that does just that:

> Your lips are dark, my love,
> and fleshy, like a date
> And night is honeyslow
> in coming, long to wait—
> I have fasted, darling,
> daylong all Ramadan—
> but your mouth—so sweet,
> so near—the hours long!
> Grant but one taste—one kiss!
> You know what good reward
> feeders of fasters gain
> from our clement Lord—
> See how the fruits are ripe
> and ready, O servant of God—
> Kiss me—it's time, it's time!
> And let us earn reward

Titled "More Than One Way to Break a Fast," this poem utilizes dashes, trimeter lines, and rhyme reminiscent of Emily Dickinson. The poem's coyness and witty eroticism hearken also to Marvell and Sidney. This ironic but self-conscious intertextual practice falls neatly into Kahf's aim to make the Muslim visibly and audibly recognizable in, and thus native to, the West. To better understand the poem, however, the reader will need to remember that during Ramadan, practicing Muslims abstain from food, drink and all forms of eroticism from dawn to sunset. Following a religious tradition, Muslims break their fast with dates, the famed fruit of the desert. The poet wants a kiss, which according to the poem's title is another way to break a fast, thus shifting the poem's focus to the sexual rather than nutritional deprivation experienced in Ramadan. But who could the speaker's "love" be? The poem is open enough for a Western reader to think it is simply her lover, or even a female partner. Its purpose is perhaps to show Islam as a faith where piety and sexuality are harmonized, which is a stretch by all accounts.

Kahf's poem is intriguing in other ways. The poem hides its piety behind coy lustfulness; it does manage to challenge the predominant mind-sets of both Muslims and non-Muslims. For pious Muslims who may find the poem risqué, the poet manages to assert that female desire can be expressed and even celebrated. After all, our speaker had been fasting all day, and her choice of how to break her fast is her own business. For a non-Muslim reader, unaware of the poem's flirtation with piety, the portrait of a lustful Muslim female helps undermine the stereotype of the sexually repressed Muslim woman, and that can only be good for all concerned, but especially for Muslim women.

So focused is Kahf on representing Muslims to outsiders and on empowering Muslim women, we never quite get a sense of what it's like to be a Muslim when not on display. Gifted with a sense of humor and comfortable with hipster idiom, Kahf also uses bravado and bombast to express pride in her Muslim history, as in the poem "By the Gates of Alhambra." These tones, however, often shield us from understanding the Muslim experience. Like ancestral praise songs, they are not meant to be questioned and can be really enjoyed only by the children of the ancestors. The poet, nonetheless, recognizes the limits of religion as a source of identity. In one of the most compelling poems in the collection, "Learning to Pray All Over," the poet promises, "One of these days, I'll add / A spiritual dimension to my life" (97). Envisioning a form of natural religion, she adds, "Nude I will go, everywhere, out / rageous and in appropriate, reveling." Shedding traditional Muslim ways of worship along with hijab and face veil, she declares, "I will find / Rock, stream, tree, wind, road / These will become my daily prayers" (98). This poem ends Kahf's book. We will have to wait until her second volume to see what becomes of this spiritual, nonsectarian, even nontheist vision.

2.

If Mohja Kahf's women are likely to be discriminated against because of their appearance, which makes their struggle as Muslims one about surfaces, Daniel Moore, a Caucasian Muslim, has the privilege of not being detected, so he can practice his spiritual inclinations in peace. Of his two recent books, I turn to *Ramadan Sonnets*. In some ways, he is like his Puritan forefathers, for whom the experience of faith is an individual matter. Writing about Ramadan, the poet chronicles the pains, joys, and ecstasies of the fast largely on his own.

For Moore, Ramadan serves as the prism through which the poet both examines his individual faith and generates it. His work is full of allusions to infinities, multitudes, and depths. He often ponders the stars and the cosmos and laments human desecration of the environment. He meditates on the mysteries of the human body and the synergy of biology and spirituality that fasting reveals. We frequently encounter the image of miners in his poems, where the journey into the depths of the earth, with a frail light attached to one's head, provides a metaphor for a spiritual quest. A California native who led an experimental theater group in the Bay Area and befriended the original Beats, Moore seems to depend on a rich literary and visual imagination to affirm his faith. He accepts orthodox Islamic doctrine but needs his rich, even surrealistic imagination to recreate the space in which he, God and the cosmos are at peace.

The poems in *Ramadan Sonnets* point to the precarious social life of Muslims in the United States. Moore ponders the streets of America while fasting and how the world he lives in does not respond to his spiritual state. He reminisces about times lived in Muslim countries when he broke the fast with others and spent afternoons listening to his spiritual mentor in Meknes, Morocco. He attempts to recapture the sense of community that Ramadan provided him and his fellow believers through communal worship and social contact. Again, like his Puritan forebears, he finds ecstasy in individual spiritual quest but also recognizes the solitude of his being a Muslim in America, especially during Ramadan. In this regard, his work provides a subtle critique of American life and the solitude that imbues it.

Moore is attuned also to the turbulent lives of many of his fellow Muslims outside America. Palestine, Bosnia, and Iraq feature among his preoccupations. Poems that address these subjects can only serve to cement his place in the American Muslim community. We would search in vain in Moore's work for any criticism of Islam or of Muslims, as if Muslim life in America and abroad would be trouble-free if it were not for outside forces such as colonialism and racism. A sense of protectiveness for his harassed co-believers pervades his work, as well as an element of public piety. At every mention of Muhammad, he tacks on the pious phrase "peace be upon him." The phrase only slows the pace of the poetry. A similar stiffness in phrasing is reflected in Moore's formal prosodic choices. His least successful poems in *Ramadan Sonnets* are the sonnets themselves in which the poet's ecstatic quest is stifled by ready-made wisdom. In his free ranging, free verse poems, however, the poet cuts loose. In "Inestimable Water," "Drunkenness of the Word" and "The Human Tribe" self-deprecation, tender humor, anger, fear and acceptance of mortality commingle, and the poet manages to soar beyond his vast American surroundings:

> Who is this
> pert and handsome
> rogue with the rose in his
> teeth, the
> glamorous cotillion belle decked out in
> flounces, who are these
> grinning, nearfamous, utterly charming
> renegades who refuse to take the whole
> journey toward the light? What is their
> resistance, who do they paint such a
> wooden sneer on otherwise so
> pliable faces?
> Why, in the valley of
> newblown wildflowers are there
> such hard rocks glaring
> balefully at the
> sky
>
> (43)

This is Moore at his best, without formal English prosody or the Muslim idiom of piety to contain him. His lines range and bend and swirl to reach the right image and argument for the moment of inspiration. In these moments of lyrical expansion, as the poet searches for the appropriate metaphor for his experience of faith, his work is indeed illuminating to Muslims and non-Muslims and fully belongs to a mystical tradition that incorporates Rumi, Blake, St. John of the Cross, and Mirabai.

3.

Agha Shahid Ali, in his first book, *The Half-Inch Himalayas* (1987), underlines his Muslim origins with frequent images of prayer rugs and worshippers deep in prayer. One gets the sense that he is staging departures from his inherited faith in those early poems. Assigning prayer and scenes of religious devotion to the dead or elderly, he allocates to the past these traditional means of seeking an inner life. In the poem "In the Mountain," the poet tells us he has forgotten "every name of God," while the man who lives his life, or his double, waits with "the Koran frozen to his fingertips" (56). The poet's double is frozen to the poet's shed faith but will outlive him and await news of the poet's death. The poem suggests that the lives exiles leave behind endure and haunt them. If the poet in exile sheds emblems of faith by assigning them to the dead, his double remains attached to these emblems. Ali portrays a Muslim's exile as a kind of Sisyphean enterprise: the poet attempts to move the solid rocks of his faith but instead creates a mountain of nostalgia. Appropriately, when Ali turned his attention to America, he titled his second book *A Nostalgist's Map of America* (1991), confirming that much of what he brought with him is remembered experience that refuses to adhere to the present and refuses to vanish.

In *Nostalgist* and the volume that follows it, *The Country without a Post Office* (1997), Ali's personal concerns broaden into a cultural panorama. Ali returns to his native Kashmir in *The Country without a Post Office* to respond to the violence there. A cursory look at the epigraphs of the poems shows a variety of influences and inspirations (Yeats, Tacitus, Shakespeare, Herbert, Hope, Hopkins, Mandelstam, and Dickinson), and one epigraph is a passage from the Quran. The mixing of these sources highlights his hybrid literary genealogy. In several poems, we notice the emergence of the Quranic and biblical figure of Ishmael, grandfather of Muslims, whom the Quran tells us was Abraham's offering to God instead of Isaac. Here, Ali asserts that his allusions, if not cosmology, are Muslim. In this book, he places Kashmir alongside Palestine, Sarajevo and Chechnya, all predominantly Muslim regions whose struggles for liberation are supported by Muslims worldwide. In addition, a Muslim to Muslim conversation that is meant to be overheard by a non-Muslim gives the poem "Hans Christian Ostro" its form and content. The poem is an elegy for a German tourist who was kidnapped and killed in Kashmir. Here, Ali turns to Muslim tradition to decry the innocent man's murder. "Whoso gives life to a soul shall be as if he had to all of mankind given life" goes the Quranic passage referenced in the poem, which also contains its reverse: "Whoso ever has taken life from a soul shall be as if he had taken life from all mankind" (86). Ali condemns the grave violation by his fellow Kashmiris of the faith they purport to defend and attempts to absolve Islam of being the inspiration of such crimes.

Ali's *Rooms Are Never Finished*, published as the poet was dying in 2001, fuses the political, personal, and spiritual into a powerful elegy. Ali found no solace in Muslim platitudes when he confronted his mother's death two years earlier. In the book's opening sequence, "From Amherst to Kashmir," he turns to the legend of the martyrdom of Imam Hussein and the lament of Hussein's sister, Zainab, to voice his grief at the loss of his mother. On Ashura, the greatest holy day in Shia Islam, believers passionately grieve the murder of Hussein by telling his story and enacting Zainab's lament. Ali's poetic sequence quotes the women accompanying Zainab. "O Muhammad," they wail, "the angels of Heaven send blessings upon you, but this is your Hussein, so humiliated and disgraced, covered with blood and cut into pieces, and your daughters are made captives, your butchered family is left for the East Wind to cover with dust" (14). The women honor the prophet of Islam but are dumbfounded by God's injustice. "How could God allow this to happen?" they ask (25). Ali's poem turns in anger at God, declaring, "God is the only assassin" (44). The poet makes religious legend personal by positioning himself as the grieving Zainab and his mother as the martyred Hussein.

"From Amherst to Kashmir" is ambitious, as it carries the burden of a double elegy. But it is not the best of Ali's work. When alluding to Muslim symbols or history, Ali is at his best when he is aware that an outsider is listening. Not burdened by the defensiveness that colors Kahf's and Moore's work, his references to Muharram, Ashura, and even martyrdom have a natural ease about them, an ease that we notice in the poetry practiced in Muslim countries and directed at Muslims. Self-identified as an exile, Ali wrote poems that meant to disarm outsiders by his mastery of English verse and his ability to make the exotic familiar or even inevitable. In "From Amherst to Kashmir," however, his desire to make the metaphor of mother as victim or martyr forces him to pile on cultural references, thus displacing the personal grief. When grief does voice itself, it comes out in high-pitched cries. The problem faced here is not specific to Islamic allusions; it is the ability or inability of myth to express personal trauma. Images of Ashura in a Shiite context resonate with viscerally impacting emotion; it is perhaps this powerful inheritance, which the poet was unable to shed, that proved nontransferable to outsiders in his elegy.

Though more imaginative and daring in its use of Islamic references, Ali's passionate reversal of myth into raw, secular grief recalls some of Kahf and Moore's strategic approaches. To varying degrees, the poets presented here do not take Islam's dicta at face value. Kahf turns a declaration of piety into a scene of seduction, albeit within the parameters of propriety. Moore's wild, surrealist-inspired visualizations assert that orthodox belief and practice require as much active imagination as they do discipline, and imagination is a quality that most orthodox believers in most religions do their best to suppress. Islamic traditions in the hands of these poets offer ample opportunities for poetry. But to what end?

To ask what is aimed also demands that we know the context where these aims are devised. Ali's use of the martyrdom of Hussein to elegize his mother would be seen in the Muslim world's generally secular literary scenes as audacious in the way that a twenty-first century Western poet using the passion of Christ for the same purpose would seem preposterous. The use of Islamic allusions in the works of Kahf and Moore would seem somewhat heavy-handed. However, the use of these allusions in the context of American poetry plays a large role in establishing these Muslim poets' claim to distinction and innovativeness. That most of their audiences are slow to decipher their allusions provides our poets with opportunities to be both heretical and traditional without the burden that these categories entail. The Islamic allusions they incorporate are integral to their poetic visions, which are based on living on the margins of both the United States and the Muslim world at large. These allusions emerge from a desire to belong as well as from a desire to promote tolerance and understanding. Reading these works, we can be comforted by the fact that poetry brooks no orthodoxy and that, while our poets are conscious of their alterity, their poetry is, at its best, comfortable in its alien skin.

Works Cited

Ali, Agha Shahid. *The Country without a Post Office.* New York: Norton, 1997.
Ali, Agha Shahid. *The Half-Inch Himalayas.* Hanover: Wesleyan University, 1987.
Ali, Agha Shahid. *A Nostalgist's Map of America.* New York: Norton, 1991.
Ali, Agha Shahid. *Rooms Are Never Finished.* New York: Norton, 2002.
Kahf, Mohja. *E-Mails from Scheherazad.* Gainesville: University Press of Florida, 2003.
Kahf, Mohja. "More Than One Way to Break a Fast." *Post Gibran: Anthology of New Arab American Writing.* Munir Akash and Khaled Mattawa, eds. Syracuse: Syracuse University, 1999. 263.
Moore, Daniel. *Ramadan Sonnets.* San Francisco: Kitab/City Lights, 1996.

Translation Impossible

Some people still recall the brilliant controversial Polish-American novelist, Jerzy Kosinski, author of the National Book Award winning novel, *Steps*; the remarkable *Being There*, which was made into an excellent film; and the unforgettable and harrowing *The Painted Bird*. The young Kosinski and his parents survived the Holocaust due to the cunning of his father and the generosity and bravery of fellow Polish nationals.

Kosinski migrated to the United States in 1957 while his parents stayed in Poland. He tells the story of telephone conversations he had with his father, who was a classicist, and how the two of them tried to talk in Latin, which the junior Kosinski also knew. As they spoke, they used to hear clicks and chirps, signs of the authorities listening in to their conversation. Then one day, the operator barged in and declared, "This call must be terminated. You are speaking in a language that is not recognized by the United Nations!" Click.

The amusing thing about the Kosinski anecdote is also what is frightening about it. One can imagine a scene in a film showing the translators' corps working for the Polish secret police calling on each other, those on duty and those off, or others on vacation, trying to find the one who specializes in this strange language—all the languages recognized by the United Nations. It's a special joy to see those in power befuddled by the things they're supposed to have mastered. In the end, the Polish secret police ended the Kosinskis' conversation because they could not filter them. Like all smart customs regulators trying to catch smugglers, they have to let some things get through if they are ever going to catch the big one. But what happens when they cannot see or understand what they are certain is passing before them? That's when they step in and stop the traffic altogether.

Let me now turn to another extreme example that involves another translation of invasive languages and what to allow in. The antiterror apparatuses in the Pentagon and the CIA/NSA have a dream of doing away with their native language experts (their middle men) and replacing them with translation machines that will translate accurately, without bias or mediation. They have set up phone interceptors to listen to telephone calls from all over the world, specifically to listen in for terrorist language. They have given their machines certain words in Arabic, such as "Jihad" and "the Great Satan" to catch potential plotters. This is what America is listening for. How many terrorists/jihadists ever mention Jihad in their phone conversation, I don't know.

The point about the two cases mentioned is that translation constantly rubs against our notions of Utopia. One of these versions involves a translator who provides information so perfectly that we are overjoyed by the union of languages. This is a dream in which two languages come together and where the translator is supposed to dissolve. People want this to happen in translation so much that even those who do not understand a language are often willing to correct or question the translator. That's what happens when you translate so well. People want to shove you aside and speak to each other directly! But a translator or translation is not like a judge or minister presiding over a marriage union whom everyone forgets after the wedding. Translation sticks around and so makes us conscious of our reality.

There's also the utopian vision that Walter Benjamin suggested in his "The Task of the Translator." Benjamin preferred that translation be literal, and in that way imperfect, so it points to an ideal of poetry that exists beyond the work translated. Translation should try to capture "an idea in the mind of God," he wrote, an idea that we can't reach in our own language, and that no language or no poetry can express. Translation, according to Benjamin's suggestion, should make us realize that we have been engaged in a kind of suspension of disbelief as to our poetic inadequacy. He wanted translation to lead us to the ruins of a linguistic utopia, to Babel before the tower was built and when we had one language. He also meant for translation in this manner to make us imagine an afterlife where an ideal of beauty and transparency dominates.

Is translation possible? I do not like the verb "is" in this question, nor do I like the adjective "possible"? I feel that the question posed before us is ontological: Is this a chair? Yes, it is a chair. That's not a good question. Let's try again: A stuffed tiger and a living tiger are both tigers; it is the active verbs that tell us which of them lives and which merely exists. To try to harness the living noun of translation with a verb like "is" will only strangle it. Translation is never *is*, translation happens, it does. And if an adjective is needed, the first I can think of here is "inevitable."

So if translation is inevitable, how do you deal with it? The Polish secret police's answer is one way. In Libya when the Qaddafi regime was in power and noted some suspicious activity, it kept only the land lines open, and there to, only foreign-language phone calls that the government could translate were allowed to continue. During the uprising that brought down the regime, it shut down the mobile phone network altogether, which was very difficult to do since even their own people needed cell phones. Such limitations are not practical in America, where the phone lines need to be open for the system to work. The CIA/NSA's solution to the chaos that translation causes is another utopian vision of sorts, an electronic tower of Babel that intercepts and translates all the foreign language calls coming through.

The CIA/NSA phone intelligence people and their dream are an extreme example, but the point is that the act of trawling, to fish out what we expect to hear, is not limited to governments. And the issue is not limited to catching the so-called bad apples. Only yesterday, a fellow poet and I wondered why two of the best-selling poets in America are an Arab and an Iranian (Kahlil Gibran and Rumi) who hail from America's great enemy regions. Also two of the best-selling novels in recent years have been by an Afghani, Khaled Husseini. What are we listening for when we read/translate works by our sworn enemies?

Is translation possible? Translation will happen, but what do we do when what comes before us defies our expectations like Kosinski's Latin? In what sense do we set up magnets to seek out certain vibrations, tones, and phrases from those speaking other languages? In what way does translation exclude, and what does it include—and how? More than any other kind of exchange, translation seems to me the route through which cultural goods are exchanged—in fact, where sometimes cultural goods flee into another language so that they are protected. Indeed, languages can serve as preservatives for cultural products outside of them or what Benjamin called an afterlife. There is a whole body of Moroccan literature that is preserved in English now—I'm referring to Paul Bowles's work—that does not exist in Arabic. There are endless ethnographic accounts of thousands of people speaking other languages preserved in European languages. There are the forced confessions of Abu Ghraib and Guantanamo too. I have a feeling that the translations exist, but the originals are deeper in the files.

The other side of this equation is how not translating can be a form of safety. It's common now in Arab countries, like Egypt, at Christmas to see Santa Claus and the phrases "Merry Christmas" plastered all over the place even in shops that do no cater to tourists. Kept in its own language, "Merry Christmas" is a quaint, foreign thing. There are Christians in Egypt and what they say to each other in Arabic about Christmas is not often heard on the street. I mean "Merry Christmas" does not threaten Egyptian Muslims when it stays un-translated. The words "St. Valentine's Day" could not be translated as such in Saudi Arabia because of the Christian reference and a general aversion to sainthood in Wahhabi Islam. So the holiday has become "the Feast of Love." The holiday is so popular among young people in Saudi Arabia that the government had to intervene. Perhaps the young Saudis will start calling it something else, since celebrating love or sainthood is not allowed in their country.

The point is that translation, however invisible, often rubs against currents of power. It runs into trouble and it causes trouble. I think also, that as a counterweight to utopia, translation happens in perpetuity; there's no stasis in it as in all utopian visions. Babel merely existed before the tower was built. It was all that noise in the tower that gave Babel its allegorical name. And if signs are at play in one language, deviating from their assigned meanings, watch what they'll do when they couple with other signs from another language. A feast of love, indeed. Translation goes on, and requires several attempts, embodying the doubling of noise, the yes and no of our exchanges. It also includes the moment of anticipation in which the words coming at us and the words we anticipate in our mouths are wrestling, corroding, combining. We let what is outside of us settle within, and claim an equal portion of the other's generosity.

I love Kosinski's story because it highlights how the powers that be recognize translation's inevitable subversiveness, and that is why, to me, it serves as a sign of a culture's brain wave activity, how translation is like water, and, in that sense, it is the best means of finding cracks in a society's dead matter, its hard-core notions. The Polish example is one system's response to plug all the holes, and we know what happened to that. And like air translation corrodes nonliving matter that does not organically engage it—from iron to rust, and from rust to dust, to Whitman's handkerchief of the Lord, a new language/word is born.

Epic Temptations
On an Unwritten Poem

In late December 1990, I called the cable company and canceled my subscription. In previous months, I caught myself too frequently watching until the same infomercial was broadcast simultaneously on three channels. I was developing an addiction, an overwhelming desire to keep up with the news of the upcoming war. Though the infomercials were a kind of antidote to Ted Koppel's blatant anti-Arab posturing, Carson's Sodom/Saddam one-liners, and the general approval—from Bob Hope to Bob Dylan—of the establishment's version of what needed to be done to Iraq, I knew I needed to give up television altogether, at least until the war ended, and the subsequent media blitzes passed on.

I was in Cairo when Iraqi troops invaded Kuwait. Like many people there, I accepted the "U.N." effort and the strong international response. I knew the West acted quickly only because Kuwait has important oil reserves (because Kuwait is not Cambodia or East Timor); but I also knew that Saddam Hussein was a vicious man, and the idea of the world gathering strength to squash his totalitarian regime appealed to me and gave me some hope. My sense of hope, though, was ironic. I was counting on people's inability to contain the repercussions of their actions.

Months before the invasion of Kuwait, we witnessed, on television, how a crowd at the West German consulate in Vienna triggered the collapse of the Soviet Bloc. Maybe the same could happen in the Middle East, I thought. Maybe the Kuwait war would expose the brutal nature of all the Middle East regimes and the tremendous oppression under which millions of people existed.

My assessment of the events in Kuwait changed within weeks of my return to the United States. On the radio and television, reporters did not question the war's purpose but, instead, referred to pundits who, in so many words, declared the current conflict a natural byproduct of the inherently violent "Arab mind." On the streets, there were the grotesque displays of patriotism and the Arab bashing—mosque burnings, bomb threats, beatings of Arab Americans—events that never made the news. Then there was a long telephone conversation with an Arab friend who said, "The Arabs must learn to accept their small place in the world." This stunned me. I had heard many Arabs express self-deprecating, even self-loathing, remarks about their race and nationality. I understood these remarks as angry expressions arising from a people's inability to achieve their ambitions, but I never heard resignation such as my friend's. Did my friend's attitude result from living in America and from being exposed to the U.S. media and government propaganda? Though directed at the American public, could the propaganda have led a proud Arab such as my friend to feel inferior? I did not know then, and I still don't know the answer to these questions. I did, however, know that the gap between my friend's attitude and mine, and the even larger gap between my attitude and that of the majority of the people of the country in which I have chosen to live, these gaps demanded an explanation, a bridging, and an epic of sorts. I called the cable company and canceled my subscription. I sat down to write.

1.

Maybe not an explanation but a response to the dehumanization of the people I had grown up amongst and to whom I still belong, a people who have been stereotyped "as incompetent boobs, forever fumbling with their fezzes, or bloodthirsty primitives . . . backward, scheming, fanatic terrorists who are dirty, dishonest, oversexed and corrupt" (Ghareeb 17). It was difficult not to take these representations of Arabs personally, and it was as a person, not as a spokesman of a tribe, that I wanted to speak. The representations of the Arabs were a lie and I knew something better, something closer to the truth. As an artist, though, I distrusted quick reactions. An artistic endeavor must grow beyond its initial stimuli for it to endure and for it to become art.

Though I am primarily a poet, I still tried not to limit my options to that genre. Because of the nature of the epic, I felt I could "explain" by means of collage, using various narratives rather than one. Poetry allows for this as well as for an autobiographical narrator historian, a kind of first-person omniscient voice. I wanted to be able to use dramatic monologues and dialogues, direct address, and stream of consciousness; I wanted to quote religious texts, history texts, official documents, diaries, poems, popular songs, proverbs, and jokes. This kind of integration, a modern version of the epic, would be the only way to convey what Georg Lukacs called "the extensive totality of life" (Lukacs 46) that I wanted to convey.

The goals and approach I set for the poem would have easily disqualified it from what has been traditionally known as "epic." Ezra Pound asserts that "an epic cannot be written against the grain of its time . . . the writer must voice the general heart," (quoted in Bernstein 19). I was not about to voice the general American heart; I was hoping to change it. The poem I had in mind would violate the general conception of an epic as "a narrative of its audience's own cultural, historical, or mythic heritage" (Bernstein 14), the "tale of the tribe" told by one of its members. Yes, I do consider myself a de facto member of the American tribe, but I am also a member of another tribe. I intended to write a poem that would introduce one people to another, a function that was never associated with the epic. The epic addresses the citizen, "not the individual in his absolute inwardness" (Bernstein 14) to reaffirm values that the citizen believes at some level. It is largely this belief in citizenship that has led most Americans to support unquestioningly the Iraq war and many others before it. I wanted to address the individual, to emphasize human commonalities rather than cultural or national differences. Furthermore, a sense of hope and heroism are associated strongly with the epic. Pound wrote that "for forty years I have schooled myself . . . to write an epic which begins 'In the Dark Forest,' crosses the Purgatory of human error, and ends in light" (quoted in Merchant 87). Considering the war that was taking place at the time, the story I wanted to tell then was more an act of desperation than hope. As for heroes, an epic is "considered a storehouse of heroic examples and precepts by which later generations would measure their own conduct" (Bernstein 8). I did not wish to employ this feature of the epic because it points to "central character[s] of station and stature performing heroic deeds" (Miller 24). I did want to employ characters endowed with exceptional abilities but whose universal humanity is demonstrated and emphasized by their common aspirations. Two questions remained unanswered: Why was it necessary to write an epic? Is it not possible to write poetry about history without the epic form? Yes, it is possible to write poems about history without the epic form. But for lyric poetry, history for the most part, is a kind of ruse, a tactic used to illustrate philosophical assertions. I did not want to use history; I wanted to write it. I chose epic precisely because it is the best poetic form of writing history, as for many peoples, epics were, and to some degree still remain, the only sources of their histories. Even though I wanted to address an audience unfamiliar with the background of my story, I was still interested in telling a tale of my tribe, to use Pound's definition. The epic muse, more tolerant and flexible than the novel's, still asks the poet: Where is this leading to, and how does this part contribute to the overall construct of the poem? The flexibility of lyric poetry and the linear narrative drive of the epic created a loose combination in which I believed I could take risks and digress and still have a shed to rest in. Having established an understanding of the kind of epic poem I wanted to write, all I had to do then was begin.

2.

Sitting down to write, I had no second thoughts about limiting the scope of the poem to my native Libya. It is a place about which I know more about than other Arab countries. There were enough complexities in Libya's modern history to demonstrate the falsehood of any generalization or stereotype about Arabs and Muslims in general. I felt comfortable beginning with the premise that Libya's history "is part of the long human rights struggle toward freedom" (Hayden 75). In V. S. Naipaul's terms, I was moved to write by trying "to understand how my corner of the [world] . . . capable of developing any number of ways, had become the place it was" (49). Even more specifically, I wanted to understand the history of my extended family in terms of the larger history of the country. I had the sense, and still do, that much of my personal history can be understood in terms of the history of modern Libya. So much of what happened to my family, so many of the major decisions we made, were direct responses to the politics of the time. Of course, one can easily overdetermine the effects of politics on personal development. For the sake of veracity, and for the work to succeed, the correspondences between personal and national history must be there. It is important that history not be presented as a kind of background music; rather, the interweaving of the personal and political history must develop into a way of seeing the world and experiencing it. In his essay "A Prologue to an Autobiography," V. S.

Naipaul explores how he came to look at the world without distinguishing between the autobiographical and historical, and how this approach was the main drive in his career as a writer. In the following passage, he explains how these issues were raised as early as the first sentence of his first novel.

> There was much in that call of 'Bogart!' that had to be examined. It was spoken by a Port of Spain Indian, a descendent of nineteenth-century indentured immigrants from South India; and Bogart was linked in a special Hindu way with my mother's family. So there was a migration from India to be considered, a migration within the British Empire. There was my Hindu family, with its fading memories of India; there was India itself. And there was Trinidad, with its past of slavery, its mixed populations, its racial antagonisms and its changing political life; once part of Venezuela and the Spanish Empire, now English speaking, with the American base and an open-air cinema at the end of Bogart's street. (32–33)

Naipaul comes full circle. He begins with Bogart and travels centuries and continents to gain an understanding of himself and his mission as a writer. The story of Bogart and Miguel Street could not be truly told without the historical, social, and political contexts. Similarly, the exploration of these contexts would be meaningless without a Bogart guiding readers through them.

Naipaul was helpful in articulating and validating my broad sense of personal history, a sense I felt necessary if I was to write an epic. But this awareness of history is not the sole domain of epic poets. C. K. Williams writes:

> the task of inserting ourselves as poets into history is something that happens not in the public world, in our lives as citizens, but in our monologues as selves. It is the most intimate activity for the poet, it is one of the most basic demands in the life of the poet. (123)

Williams's declaration validated my project by suggesting that my insertion of my story in history is part and parcel of my work as a poet. I felt that my story had as much claim to be part of human history as any other.

3.

I knew that the poem would cover the period from 1911 to the present. Nineteen eleven was the year the Italians invaded Libya to colonize the country. It made sense to begin there because that era still has it repercussions on Libya. Colonization ushered in the industrial age with its modern modes of administration, government, and systems of oppression. Before the Italians, Libya had been part of the Ottoman Empire for 400 years, and though that regime was also oppressive, the people had an allegiance to the Caliph and to the notion of a unified Muslim entity. Unlike the Turks, the Italians had little in common with the Libyans. They wanted to confiscate land and inhabit it with their own people. In 1911, my grandparents' world changed, and they had to struggle to perceive new lives and new futures for themselves. Politics began to intervene in their lives directly. In my long poem, I wanted to chronicle how they and their descendants zigzagged through historical events. For this plan to work, I needed to construct a chronology that would incorporate the history of Libya and my family's history. Yet even after sketching a chronology, I could not begin. I think I was hampered by my awareness of the enormity of the task. I needed a dramatic moment that would start the poem with the events of 1911. I thought of earlier poems I had written and found this one, which seemed like the kind of beginning I needed.

Sa'doon

My Grandmother dreams of General Graziani,
when he rode into Misrata with a peasant's head
raised on the hood of his armored car.

Earlier that day, he had driven a tank over
her brother Sa'doon.

The General raised his arms to the sky and commanded
the vultures to leave nothing behind.

On an October dawn,
in a goatskin tent near Tobruk,

she gives birth to a son,

names him Sa'doon.

The Bedouin guide taking her
to Sidi Ghazi, where
she hopes to be a peasant again,
starts a fire.

He burns branches of a date palm
that no longer gives shade or fruit.

He milks the she-camel
and sings to her
the news of
my father's
birth.

The poem seemed melodramatic, but it did illustrate the zigzagging. The story here is of my family's immigration to Egypt in 1924. By then, the Fascists were in control of the government of Italy. Mussolini reinvigorated the Fourth Shore campaign and began brutally imposing Italian control, which, until then, had been limited to major cities and towns, over the entire country. Sa'doon was my great-uncle. After he was captured and murdered, the resistance movement he led in the western region of Libya came to a halt. My family fled to Egypt, 1,200 miles away. The poem gave me a villain and a beginning. I went to the library to read Graziani's two books of memoirs, but they were not available in English. I began reading a book about the most important governor of Libya, Italo Balbo. Balbo, who fascinated me, had had an interesting life before becoming governor; he seemed charming, dynamic and good-humored; and he was not as brutal as Graziani. A poem resulted from reading Balbo's biography.

I was attracted to Balbo because of the American connection relayed in the poem, the street in Chicago named after him, his meeting with Roosevelt, and the ticker-tape parade held for him on Broadway in New York. I thought his story would create interesting parallels with the poems on my life in America. Balbo's story would have also demonstrated the most troubling side to Italian colonialism; Balbo, and even the sadistic Graziani, believed they were doing the Libyans a favor. In the poem, I wanted to catch Balbo when he was most comfortable and reveal to him, and to the reader, the misery that led to his peace of mind. The poem also served as an example of the first-person omniscient voice I wanted to develop. I felt I needed some sense of authority, however tenuous or even false, in order to continue writing the poem. But reading this passage in Segre's biography of Balbo revealed to me the real nature of Balbo's role in Libya's history:

> One of Balbo's first goals as governor was to eradicate all memory of the period of Italian repression. Italian military sovereignty over all of Libya had been secured only three years before he came to power. The tribes of Cyrenaica in particular, under the banner of the Sanussi religious order and the leadership of Omar el Mukhtar, had put up a fierce resistance. The Italians replied in kind with a ruthless campaign of summary executions, decimation of flocks, and mass internments of the nomadic populations of the Gebel. According to official Italian figures, the Cyrenaican population dropped from 225,000 in 1928 to 142,000 in 1931. (322)

Balbo came to clean up the mess left behind by Graziani. I had forgotten this fact because I was seduced into liking Balbo for his archeological site restorations, the coastal railway stretching 1,200 miles, the resort hotels he built and the Grand Prix auto-race he started. I had to leave Balbo behind and go back to Graziani and to the thousands he killed in Cyrenaica.

4.

In search of more information about Graziani, I went back to an earlier book by Segre, *Fourth Shore: Italian Colonization of Libya*. Segre is considered the best authority on the subject of the American academic scene, and his book is the most comprehensive book on Italian colonialism in North Africa. The book contains only two references to Graziani and does not mention the persecution in Cyrenaica. Another book by John Wright devotes one page to the subject. He reports that Graziani's forces killed 12,000 annually in their effort to complete the conquest of Cyrenaica (35). The figure Wright cites comes from a New York Times article published in 1945, two years after the complete Allied victory in North Africa and ten years after the genocide. A book titled *The Italian Empire: Libya*, published in 1940 by the Italian Library of Information, New York, includes no mention of the killings in Cyrenaica. Again, either the story was never reported on, or it had become so unimportant that the authors of the book had no qualms about omitting it.

This omission made the story more compelling, but I did not know where else to look. A cousin sent me a book about the trial of Omar el Mukhtar, the old man who led the fight against the Italians in Cyrenaica. This was the most informative work I had seen, and it helped me piece together the story.

After gaining complete control of the Western region of Libya in 1924, the Italians focused on Cyrenaica in the East and launched surprise attacks on various towns (Santarelli 41). The mountainous terrain allowed the natives to begin guerrilla resistance, but it would be wrong to view the genocide as simply a reaction to the resistance. Graziani had planned on "disarming the people, concentrating them, confiscating their goods" before the resistance became active (Santarelli 29–30). He wanted to confiscate lands and displace the natives who lived largely on herding, and he wanted to turn them into laborers for the Italian colonists (Santarelli 29–34). For four years, Italian forces attacked the tribes killing 1,500 men and 90,000–100,000 animals (the killing of livestock was intended to starve the natives and deprive them of their traditional way of life).

By 1929, the tribes were exhausted. The rebels called a truce and wanted to negotiate. This lasted a short while until Graziani decided to go on with crushing the resistance. The forced removal of the nomadic tribes from their grazing lands began in 1930. The tribes did support the resistance, and their removal deprived the resistance of badly needed supplies. The tribes were moved to six locations, some as far as 600 miles from their original areas. Many died on the way to the concentration camps (there are no good estimates available on this). In the camps, movement was extremely restricted, medical treatment was almost non-existent, and food was rationed. Individuals or families found outside the camps were either arrested and jailed or "hunted" (Santarelli 73). In Graziani's words, "The government is calmly determined to reduce the people to most miserable starvation" (Santarelli 78).

By 1932, practically all the livestock the tribes brought to the camps had died due to lack of water and pasture lands. Many epidemic outbreaks took place, especially exanthematous typhus. To survive, the men took jobs in the public works projects the Italians had begun building to accommodate the newly arrived colonists. They received daily wages of ten lire a day, a third of the wage given to Italian laborers. Graziani succeeded: a few months earlier he had written that he intended to make the tribes lose "the habit of nomadism and acquire the tastes and needs of sedentary populations; for it is upon these that we must necessarily found and develop our program of pacifying and exploring Cyrenaica" (Santarelli 104). Needless to say, Graziani's program worked as planned.

Through this research, I kept finding parallels with the treatment of Native Americans in the United States. I wondered about the origins of Graziani's plan. Where did this idea of the concentration camps originate? It's a well-known fact that the British were the first to construct them during the Boer wars. However, Graziani worked closely with General Badoglio, the governor of Libya before Balbo, as well as a Paolo Orano. Santarelli et al mention Orano only once in their book. Leaving Libya around 1934, Orano returned to Rome to help "solve the Jewish question in Italy" (Santarelli 30).

This was a sinister bit of information since one of the six concentration camps was considered "a punishment camp" (Santarelli 79). I wanted to know more about Orano and about his possible connections with the Nazis, a legitimate concern considering the Italian fascists' strong ties with Hitler. I wanted to know if the Libyan concentration camps with their forced labor, starvation, and punishment areas were prototypes for the Nazi concentration camps in Europe. I looked up Orano's name in various sources and found nothing. My research resulted in two villains, an unanswerable question and a mass of details, but no human angle. None of the sources I read included reactions of ordinary people, interviews with survivors, diaries, letters, anecdotes or photographs. I felt I knew "the history" well enough, but without tangible elements, I could not proceed.

5.

The void proved to be my own family's history. I went back to try to continue my father's story. I tried to remember what he had said about his childhood, and several times I asked questions to which he responded, "That was a long time ago." My ignorance frustrated me and I tried to express it in the beginning of a poem.

To His Father: A Biography

You had no life, except for your father,
talked about him as though he were

a saint. If you had any doubts about
his virtues, the three thousand mourners

who attended his funeral assured you
you should have none, and that was enough.
Still, I learned when you were twelve
your mother died giving birth to Omar.

What you remember about her follows
the same line, a loving woman, wise,
virtuous, strong. You retell the only story
I know about her: Uncle Sulaiman's eyes

were swollen "like rotten plums"
and the family could not afford
a modern doctor. Instead she followed
the advice of a feghi, heating a nail

until it became red. Grandfather told her
he could not do the piercing; So she took it
upon herself to burn the boy's temples
with the nail, his hands and feet pinned

in place by his father's strong arms.
You do not mention the cries, the fear
you must have felt, only that she was right:
Sulaiman recovered his sight in days . . .

I believe this, and will believe more
if only you would tell it. But you never will
and I am forced to tell your story
as I believe it happened . . .

    In writing the poem, I tried to piece together the early years of my father's life. Knowledge of the region's history helped me understand some of the decisions my family made. Here, knowledge of the region's history helped in constructing a biography. The poem grew to 120 lines, and though it contained many truths, it remained an incomplete fiction. I needed a gesture from my father to validate at least the emotional honesty of the poem. I asked him about a detail during a telephone conversation, and again he replied, "Oh, that happened a long time ago!" I did not pursue the question further. It is not a practice of ours to have lengthy discussions about his life, particularly on the phone. Also, after living for many years with basically all their country's phones tapped, Libyans developed a great fear of extended and detailed phone conversations. The mail would have been useless as well; my father left school in fourth grade, and my mother passed first grade but never went on. When I finally saw my parents in person, my father was suffering from kidney failure. My mother reminisced, but in light of my father's illness, was in no mood to answer my specific questions. In the face of my silence concerning the nature of my project, I had to respect her silence as well. And so for the third time, and following what I thought to be the easiest track, I came up short, this time by choice.

6.

My doubts about the epic were not unusual for any writer who embarks on a large project. Conceivably, I could have included my difficulties in writing this poem as an essential component of it. The great poets, Chaucer and Milton, make this gesture. Contemporary poets such as Walcott in *Omeros*, Peter Dale Scott in *Coming to Jakarta*, and Sharon Doubiago in *South America Mi Hija* posit themselves, though in varying degrees, as epic hero/narrators. I wanted to write an epic without being the central focus of it. But this was not the only issue that troubled me. I learned that, in order to write an epic, certain concerns must be addressed for the writing to continue.

(1) Self-Definition:

Robert Hayden explains the idea for writing "Middle Passage" came to him from a Stephen Vincent Benet poem that prophecies a poet who will write a "black-skinned epic, epic with the long black spear." Hayden said, "I dared to hope that I might be that poet" (126). Similarly, Walt Whitman "decided to cast himself in the role of his own epic hero . . . His eyes would be turned both inward and outward, and his voice would be both personal and public" (Miller 25). Whitman wrote *Leaves of Grass* with the notion of himself as the American prototypical persona. Both Hayden and Whitman mythologize themselves into the role of their audiences' spokesmen. These poets do not simply insert themselves into history; rather, they emphasize that their people's history must be processed through them. The epic poet must have a sense of self-importance, even some delusions of grandeur. I had to compensate for this by developing the first-person omniscient voice. To assume omniscience, I had to believe all the facts and fictions I wrote, and that proved too hard to sustain.

(2) Juggling History and Fiction:

Paul Merchant argues the epic poet uses historical materials for his own ends (3). I, on the other hand, wanted to write a history using poetry. The differences between these two approaches may seem artificial, considering how poetic or fictional history is. Regardless of whether the writer wants to emphasize history or fiction in the epic, the writer must possess encyclopedic knowledge of the culture she is writing about. Adrienne Rich addresses this point in the following lines:

> Suppose you want to write
> of a woman braiding
> another woman's hair—
> straight down, or with beads and shells
>
> in three-strand plaits or cornrows—
> you had better know the thickness
> the length the pattern
> why she decides to braid her hair
> how it is done to her
> what country it happens in
> what else happens in that country
>   You have to know these things
>
>   (33)

Rich demands from the writer a contextual knowledge even if one is to write a lyric. For me, the problem was the opposite. I had a broad sense of Libya's history but not enough of the details, such as the quotidian scene Rich describes. History does not give these details. And a writer will face problems if she or he tries to fill these gaps with imaginary situations. In the poem "Sa'doon," I had a bit of history: a story of a woman who gives birth while fleeing her country. I had imagined a small group of people and wrote the poem based on that. I later learned that it was a large caravan, about 2,000 people. The poem was no longer valid as history, and that, in turn, made it lose some of its artistic validity as well.

(3) Access:

So far, I have referred to the lack of the quotidian in terms of archival access—unavailability of personal testimonies, autobiographies, etc. There is also the issue of geographical access. I found it difficult to visualize scenes and speakers, having not visited Libya for fourteen years. Imagination is rooted in memory; if one's memory of a place dies, so does the ability to write imaginatively about it. In other cases in which I was not going to write poems based on memory, I needed physical access to certain settings in order to accurately describe the scenes of the poems. Places always suggest the cadence in which the poetry about them is to be written. I needed access to Libya to feel that cadence and to tell the stories according to that rhythm. Ultimately, the denial of access was in itself a psychological burden, an underlying sense of rejection by the place I wanted to write about. All these concerns raise questions about the ability of an exile to write an epic about his former country. If not impossible, the endeavor is definitely fraught with difficulties. I traveled to Cairo in the fall of 1991. The city's climate, its cadences, and the difficult circumstances I was under did not allow me to write. I found a few books on Libya's history and took many notes. One November afternoon, I tried to calculate how long it would take me to write the Libya epic. I tried also to calculate the finances of such a project, travel expenses and time off, etc. Three years, four, five? And who is willing to bankroll such an obscure project and the obscure poet who wants to undertake it? At the time, I had seven poems published, only three of which I liked. I asked myself repeatedly, "Can a poet write a good epic despite lack of finances, public interest, skill, access and reputation?" It became clear to me then that writing an epic as a first book seemed to pose more opportunities for failure than for success. I had to become a better poet and much better informed. On that November afternoon, I scribbled a few lines that had nothing to do with the epic project. I went home later and began compiling my first book manuscript. As for the epic, I would have to wait a few years, or even decades, and then begin again.

7.

After poetry readings, after lectures, and at cocktail parties, as soon as I said I was from Libya, Qaddafi's name was quickly mentioned to be followed by an unpleasant discussion of terrorism, fundamentalism, and the veil. Things are complex, I try to explain. The fanatics are bred on political and economic frustration. And while there is the veil, more women are educated and going to work and are becoming independent. What is most bothersome about these conversations is they touch on an issue central to my existence, while most of my conversation partners are so unaffected by what happens in the Arab world that holding opinions on these subjects, whether sympathetic or hostile, can be a mere intellectual exercise. These conversations always start from point zero and cover the same ground again and again. I leave these gatherings asking myself whether I am going to spend a lifetime talking like this. As a person, of course, I find this prospect an unpleasant, but still an avoidable, possibility. As a writer, on the other hand, defensiveness is an obstacle that cannot be overlooked. This kind of negative attention becomes part of one's life experience and begins to occupy one's mind. One becomes so focused on anticipating hostile remarks that he fears that every sentence he writes from then on may become a form of appeasement. The writer may make no discoveries of his or her own. Candor and expressions of vulnerability are sacrificed. And when that happens, the work begins to lose its artistic integrity.

Writing from this defensive posture, where one's mental and creative processes stoop from humility, or humiliation rather, is extremely uncomfortable. In talking with other writers of Arab origins, I found many of us share this difficulty. We all want to foster understanding of our sub-culture within the larger American scene. The Arab American community, needful of as many eloquent defenders as it could get, eggs us on in that direction. At readings of Arab American poets, members of the audience ask why no one wrote a poem about this or that violent incident. No doubt, these questions demonstrate ignorance of the artistic process. Nonetheless, they go with the territory of being an ethnic writer. To call for justice where one knows injustice is occurring is not a responsibility that other Arab American writers or I want to avoid. But injustice is not the only fact of the world. There is a nest of robins on the tree across from my window. I see the mother feeding her children, who are nothing but mouths. I know there is a universe to discover there and this moves me, yet writing about it seems a luxury. I know other Arab American writers who want to write not about what they have experienced as members of an ethnic group, or even about what they know, as the old adage suggests. But our defensiveness about our heritage has become a kind of existential state through which we experience the world. It traps us.

On a recent visit to Egypt, I had a chance to give a reading from my first book. I had dreaded this event more than any other reading, having assumed that what I have been writing about is old or no-news to Arab readers. To my surprise, the poems seemed to present a fresh look on what these readers have known or experienced. I did not need to translate the many Arabic words and phrases, an issue two American magazine editors have raised, arguing that the inclusion of Arabic may create a language barrier for their readers. In Cairo, though I read in English, I read at home. A few months later, this time in London, I read my poem to a few of my cousins from whom the word "poet" may as well be synonymous with "fool," and whose attitude towards the arts does not differ from the attitude of Arab governments who generally find art a nuisance. Yet again, the poems registered in a way I had never seen. I sensed their elation, their happiness with hearing part of their story told. It was not the glitter of bemusement that I saw in their eyes but something akin to self-recognition. The Libya epic then has to be written for them. I have become convinced that this poem will have to be written in the Arab world. An epic, now I must concur with Pound, is about continuity, about seeing living elements resonate through their connection with the past. Like ritual, this is how it nudges the present to the future. Here in the United States, the story I wanted to tell can only register as a disjointed object, like a leaf or a bone in a natural history museum. More than any other work of literature, the epic has to be written from a sense of pride. Beginning with that premise can foster candor and intimacy between poet and reader. There will be no appeal to a center that can afford to dismiss you. You are in the circle now, poet, tell us our story. I do not know if I will be the black spear that will write this poem. After all, Arabic is a kind of second language to me. Still, its rhythms crowd my head. If I were to tell my story in it, I know I will have the advantage of telling it proud, but slant.

Works Cited

Bernstein, Michael Andre. *The Tale of the Tribe: Ezra Pound and the Modern Verse Epic*. Princeton, New Jersey: Princeton University Press, 1980.

Ghareeb, Edmund, ed. *Split Vision: Arab Portrayal in the American Media*. Washington: Institute of Middle Eastern and North African Affairs, 1977.

Hayden, Robert. *Collected Prose*. Ann Arbor: University of Michigan Press, 1984.

Lukacs, Georg. *The Theory of the Novel: A Historico-Philosophical Essay on the Forms of Great Epic Literature*. Boston: MIT Press, 1971.

Merchant, Paul. *The Epic*. London: Methuen, 1971.

Miller, James E., Jr. *Leaves of Grass: America's Lyric-Epic of Self and Democracy*. New York: Twayne, 1992.

Naipaul, V. S. "A Prologue to an Autobiography." *Finding the Center*. London: Andre Deutsch, 1984.

Rich, Adrienne. *Your Native Land, Your Life*. New York: W.W. Norton, 1986.

Santarelli, Enzo, et al. *Omar Al-Mukhtar: The Italian Reconquest of Libya*, tr. John Gilbert. London: Darf Publishers, 1986.

Segre, Claudio G. *Italo Balbo: A Fascist Life*. Berkeley: University of California Press, 1987.

Williams, C. K. "The Poet and History," *Tri-Quarterly*, 72 (Spring/Summer 1988).

Wright, John. *Libya: A Modern History*. Baltimore: John Hopkins University Press, 1982.

Four Uneasy Pieces

Forerunners

an ancestry I found
among rows of dusty shelves
on yellowed sheets of fading print

eyes strain, ears strain
an impossible color, a music
seeking shelter
among borrowed storms

They tell of crazed rivers
longing to be contained
They hold the brittle words
strung together by rigid banks

They tell of austere hope
the thin line of redemption
they hoped to grasp

I hold their labors,
their cursive light
written on the air

Touching their desire
the victory in their blind pulse—
No wasted lives here. No waste

I am thinking of Toru Dutt, India's first established poet in English. Born in 1856 to a prominent Calcutta family that converted to Christianity, Dutt spent several years in France and England. At eighteen, she and her family returned to India. It was within these last three years of her life that Toru produced her work. She died of tuberculosis at the age of twenty-one in 1877. For such a young person, Toru Dutt's accomplishments are quite extraordinary. She wrote a volume of English translations of modern French poetry, a novel in French an unfinished novel in English, and *Ballads and Legends of Hindustan*, a retelling of Hindu legends in English ballad form.

Her first novel, *Le Journal de Mademoiselle d'Arvers*, is an imitation of a French romance set in 1860s France with an all-French cast of characters and written in the form of a diary. In her English novel *Bianca the Spanish Maiden*, Dutt creates a heroine modeled on herself, a dark haired, tan-skinned woman at the edge of European racial acceptability. While clearly obsessed with passing as a European, Dutt seems to have been keenly aware that she was "the same but not quite," neither in India nor in Europe. She could hardly read Bengali and only began to immerse herself in her native culture when a return to England seemed unlikely. Clearly, her acquisition of European culture so early in the cultural divide between East and West kept her unsettled at home.

Dutt's most important book is her *Ancient Ballads of Hindustan*. In this volume, which she wrote as a result of beginning a serious study of Sanskrit, she renders various Hindu legends and concludes the work with several of her own poems. While in her translations of French poetry Dutt attempted to remain true to the originals, in these Indian ballads she completely retells the ancient lays, altering their narrative lines and their thematic concerns to suit her contemporaneous social and philosophical struggles. Outlining a vision of India that stems from her hybrid mindset, she foresees her nation as democratic, monotheistic and reliant on her spiritual richness rather than Europe's science. In other poems, she waves an indignant dismissal at the original Sanskrit tales and goes on to give interpretations of them that belie the contradictions between her liberal secular leanings and her Christian faith.

The discrepancies between the book's assigned responsibility as a transmittal of Indian culture to the West and the poet's own probing raises legitimate questions. What could be the purpose of this interrogation of Hindu legends, and who is the audience for such a reassessment of the poet's native culture? Was Dutt committing an act of cultural betrayal? Is this betrayal inherent in the process of writing in another language, and in the language of the colonizer at that? These are valid questions. But they can become mere rhetorical postures that end debate rather than create openings for discussions. These questions can take a vociferous turn in the Arab world because at the nationalist level, we have particularly strong attachments to our languages, and at a deep-structural religious level, we still adhere to the spiritual superiority of Arabic.

Dutt's case is suggestive precisely because writing in another language is sometimes the only way to pose certain questions or take certain attitudes. Languages are rationales, and when we use them, we think along the grooves they make for us by the force of their histories and their intellectual output. They can lead us to paths we have not traveled before, not because of a necessarily unavoidable ideological logic, but rather by the sheer reality of their irrational technicalities, their random signification and metaphorical formations. Roman Jakobson has reportedly said that one can say anything in any language, but some languages force one to say certain things in a certain way. That "certain way," I am convinced, can make all the difference. Thinking in another language can be useful. And the so-called acts of cultural betrayal can be allegories of the cave, revelations, and epiphanies.

But— and here is the other side of the cliff—epiphanies for whom? Dutt's case demonstrated a long time ago, and the writing of many postcolonial writers still demonstrates, that writing in another (meaning European) language limits one's audience to the advantaged classes of one's culture, many of whom want to have writers as tokens of achievement but do not bother digest the criticism these writers pose. If Arabs who write in English or French now wonder about audience, we can only imagine the limited scope Dutt saw for herself during the Raj's golden age. The more palpable, current process of globalization and the existence of cosmopolitan audiences all over the world, whom Arab writers think understand them, do not provide the answer. The global cultural current, we must concur, has been a largely one-way stream for a long time. The exoticizing aspects that developed through Orientalism to assure hegemony of colonized lands and peoples are the same traps used now to commodify contemporary Arab or Eastern literature. Unfortunately, not many postcolonial writers living abroad have managed to present their cultures without the veneer of exoticism. Like Dutt, who vacillated between a romantic adoration of her country's spirituality and an Enlightenment assessment of it as irrational, many postcolonial writers seem incapable, when writing in English or French, to escape those sensationalistic trappings. At best, they are forming new mutations of Negritude.

I think it is very proper to aim widely, to address the center. But the path the trans-lingual writer takes is full of compromises, some of them necessary, some immensely useful. Writing from this outsider's perspective no agency can be shaped without keeping a cold eye fixed on one's marginalization.

I am thinking of Manmohan Ghose, also born to an elite Bengali family, in 1869. When Manmohan was ten, he, along with his two brothers Kumar and Aurobindo (known later as the poet pundit Sri Aurobindo), were sent to England to study. In 1890 at Cambridge, Ghose and three young English poets published an anthology of their verse that received favorable reviews, including one from Oscar Wilde, who commended Ghose for his quick "Oriental mind." By then, Ghose had established a reputation as a young poet of promise and was hoping to pursue a literary career in England. Without any real associations with his native land, he thought of himself as "four fifth Englishman." When his attempts to acquire a post in the British Civil Service failed, he returned to Calcutta in 1893, having lost most of his native Bengali. At home, he quickly began to feel as an "exile," and from thereon considered himself "denationalized" in a marked contrast from his two brothers who went on to lead militant nationalist movements. Ghose began teaching English literature and made a career of it. He married a woman who hardly spoke English. I see him gazing at the books of classical art reproductions he adored, evoking the Greco-Roman myths that so moved him, totally oblivious of India's legions of gods. Ghose pined for England most of his time in India. His last and closest attempt to return to London failed when the English bank where he held his life's savings went bankrupt. Almost blind, he died a broken man in 1924 at the age of fifty-four.

Noted for his lyrical touch, Ghose focused most of his energy on epic poems he never completed. For sixteen years, he worked on a tale of the Greek legend of Perseus; he was attracted to this myth because it was foretold that a poet from the East would write his story. Ghose's *Perseus The Gorgon Slayer* is full of layered allusions and similes, but so laden is the poem with Victorian bombast, convoluted diction and syntactical dismembering that it is hardly readable. His incomplete play *Nollo and Damayanti*, written in Shakespearean language, is taken from the Mahabharata. Like Dutt, Ghose alters the legend, minimizing the powers of the gods and introducing more modern themes. His version displaces much of the Hindu norms and precepts that the original version attempts to convey. Ghose's last attempt at the long poem was titled *Adam Alarmed in Paradise*. The poem was written in response to the devastation and spiritual crisis of the First World War. Yet as Adam, the Englishman protagonist, rediscovers Christ in the Himalayas, India, its people and culture, colonialism and the scramble for territories and markets that instigated the war have no bearing whatsoever on the poem. The poem was clearly not addressed to an Indian audience, not even an Anglo-Indian one. It was an attempt to respond to a horror that the author encountered from a great distance, a crisis he clearly could not fully appreciate, and therein lies the poem's failure.

This denial of India is consistent in Ghose's other works. In an elegiac sequence written to his wife, he never mentions India, never draws on Indian locale, custom, language, symbols, or landscape. Nor does he mention his wife's name, preferring to call the sequences "Immortal Eve." The poems are set in a generic romantic landscape that draws heavily on the poet's memory of England.

The poet is engaged in a negotiation with polarities, finding himself repeatedly torn between two opposing worlds. In the poem, "London," the poet is torn between an old love for nature and the excitement and human company in the urban world. He writes the poem after having chosen the urban world, but the city's feature attraction for the poet is more than just a place of connection with others. There is a subtle reference to the poet's life in England as an Indian who is in love with London and her people but finds himself a "weary," "lone spirit" longing for human connection and unable to achieve it. He attempts to resolve this sense of isolation by heading to his native India, which he calls in another poem "that far south." In that poem, called "Home Thoughts," the poet is aware that his return will be painful, and that it will take time for him to find peace. He resolves to begin shaping from his positive experiences in England a vision of his future at home. Yet, he ends the poem believing he is not likely to keep constant to his resolution. The "truth" he reminds himself of his "sighs would fain unlearn." The poet clearly anticipated his pining for England and his deeply entrenched and isolating nostalgia.

Ghose's traumatic attachment to England is not unique. His

sense of unbridgeable distance from his beloved England is no longer applicable to us today, at least not in the same way, and not for the same reasons. Ghose's case, however, points to a language's inability to thrive outside its borders. The English used in India at his time was a totally borrowed language. The Indians who spoke it, living as they were under an intolerant colonial administration, were much focused on correct mimicry of proper English than on forging their own independent forms of expression in the language. While mimicry, as Homi Bhabha notes, has the potential for menace, this aspect was not exploited. The mimicry Ghose practiced was of an assimilative type whose practitioners acknowledged their inferiority and subordination. Like other forms of imported products, the importers lagged behind and waited for the language to come their way to use it. During the Victorian era, before the advent of free verse, the gap between English poetry and its colonial imitators was, at least formally, close. Modernism, which must have seemed like a shock to Indian poets writing in English, basically shut down the business of Indian poetry in English for a good four decades. With Pound, Eliot, H. D. and the War poets, it was impossible to write the genteel lyric or the unperturbed classically inspired epic that Ghose aimed for. William Carlos Williams said that with (his version) of Modernism, "Noble" became "No Bull!" I doubt if Ghose could have understood that in India. But while in England, as the poem "London" clearly shows, Ghose had already begun to see the limitations of Romanticism and to express dissatisfaction with it. The Wordsworthian appreciation of nature seemed to him an austere, exclusive, and self-righteous stance that not everyone can appeal to. At the time, he was within a milieu that used the language freely and that attempted to dictate the terms of their composition, not have those terms be dictated to them

This boldness is what distinguishes any cultural center in any of the arts. Artistic vitality emerges from both a sense of ambition and a realization that one's surroundings and perceptions are central and worthy of representation. In terms of perception, it means that the work of art, whether of a realistic or symbolic representation, takes its genesis from one's immediate experience and surroundings. In terms of language, it means that the text has to acknowledge the language one hears and uses, accepting its quirks, innovativeness, and sense of play. If literature in general implies peculiar uses of language, this demand needs to be fulfilled much more by writers using a language outside its main realms. Works such as Amos

Tutoula's *Palm Wine Drinkard*, Chinua Achebe's *Things Fall Apart* and Derek Walcott's poetry are successful because of the liberties they take with the language. English did not make any demands on them; they wielded it any way they pleased. Herein lies their success, and Ghose's anguish.

I am thinking of Sol Plaatje, author of *Muhodi*, Africa's first novel in English published in 1930. Also author of *Mafeking Diary*, a war eyewitness account and *Native Life in South Africa*. Plaatje worked primary in journalism, through which he wrote tirelessly articulating a vision of justice and racial cooperation to forestall the violence he foresaw in his native land. Born in 1876, Plaatje was a pioneer in the history of the South African Black press and a leading founder of the South African Native National Congress, later known as the African National Congress. For many years, he worked as a translator in the colonial court system and was instrumental in preserving the Tswana language and its literature. At his death in 1932, Plaatje left behind a large correspondence, many reports submitted to government commissions, and numerous speeches in which he combined his political passions and literary skills.

As an interpreter in the British court system (he spoke several African languages in addition to Dutch and German), Plaatje was fully aware that "The administration of justice in South Africa is something different from the same thing in Europe, where judge, plaintiff, defendant, counsel and witnesses all speak the same language." The colonial court system was inconsistent and miserly about the use of translation. This was a serious matter for Plaatje. Without adequate translation, African defendants' lives hung in the balance according to how their words or the courts' were interpreted. For Plaatje, good translators were essential for justice in a multilingual society. Judges who were not linguists, he felt, could not adjudicate fairly. Linguistic expertise was necessary to lessen the weight the colonial language exerted on the colonial subjects. Plaatje explains that an African defendant usually gave a long answer in his own defense that neither confirmed nor denied his guilt. He adds, "What the prisoner really meant is that he is 'not guilty'; but his notion . . . is that to say so in two words in reply to a charge in which the British crown contends against him, is tantamount to calling his sovereign lord King Edward the Seventh— whom God preserve— a liar" (Plaatje 59). Good translators understood the colonial subject's subordinated position and made "use of their own knowledge of the circumstances [to] add such missing links not expressed by the witness" (53).

I believe it is important to remember this history of the interaction with the colonial language no matter where the colonial writer is writing. The defendants, these grandparents of ours, are only four or five generations in the past. While the power configuration with the colonialism is different now, and even though that colonial language may have become our, and sometimes our only, language, the fact remains that we are living in translation just like Plaatje's defendants. Postcolonial writing in English generally assumes the existence of another language whether the author makes the presence of that ghost language felt or not. When the postcolonial writer uses English or French, he or she is not writing from point zero. Rather she or he is inscribing on a palimpsest of his native language.

Translation as a paradigm for postcolonial literature can be very useful for approaching the subject, whether as a creative writer or a critic. As Plaatje pointed out, conveyance has its consequences. And inaccurate portrayals are acts of bad translation. By "inaccurate," I do not mean negative or critical. However, in the presence of another language, the writer may slack or simplify one's self or one's cultural background. Thinking as a translator, the postcolonial writer using another language should, as Plaatje suggests, use his "knowledge of circumstances" and add "missing links." One, both as writer or critic, needs to be aware that a complicated act of transmittal is taking place and approach the material with great attention to nuance. Postcolonial texts in European languages as acts of translations sometimes do justice to the world they depict, sometimes come short and sometimes find innovative solutions to express certain aspects.

Living in translation, while it carries responsibility with it, does open all kinds of avenues for creative use of the language. Early postcolonial writers sometimes used literal translation to add "local color." Many Indian and African writers in English have tended to limit literal translation in terms of proverbs and folktales, thus, unwittingly emphasizing their cultures' primitivism. However, taken seriously, literal translation of one's native language can invigorate one's use of the borrowed language. Attempting to convey the more complicated and more specific aspects of one's culture with a spirit of rigor and accuracy can forge new ways of thinking by the sheer freshness of the new phrases.

Yet again, as Plaatje's career demonstrates, such cultural trafficking should not go in one direction. Translating in court, he had to navigate between three or four languages, making sure everyone understood the proceedings in his or her language. In addition to his books in English, Plaatje also translated numerous works, particularly Shakespeare's, to his native Tswana. Writing in another language may not simply be a matter of choice. Rather, as Plaatje's career demonstrates, making one's output somehow available in one's native language is necessary for a sense of artistic purpose and personal wholeness. It makes the uncontainable self rove in a wide, expansive world and not feel endlessly adrift from its birthplace.

Echo & Elixir

Cairo's taxi drivers speak to me in English.
I answer, and they say your Arabic is good.
How long have you been with us? All my life
I tell them, but I'm never believed.
They speak to me in Farsi, speak to me in Greek,
and I answer with mountains of gold and silver,
ghost ships sailing the weed-choked seas.
And when they speak to me in Spanish,
I say Moriscos and Alhambra.
I say Jews rescued by Ottoman boats.
And when they speak to me in Portuguese,
all my life I tell them, coffee, cocoa,
Indians and poisoned spears.
I say Afonsso king of Bikongo writing
Manuel to free his enslaved sons.
And Cairo's taxi drivers tell me
your Arabic is surprisingly good.
Then they speak to me in Italian,
and I tell them how I lay swaddled
a month's walk from here. I tell them
camps in the desert, barbed wire, wives
and daughters dying, camels frothing disease,
the sand stretching an endless pool.
And they say so good so good.
How long have you been with us?
All my life, but I'm never believed.
Then they speak to me in French,
and I answer Djamila, Leopold, Stanley,
baskets of severed hands and feet.
I say the horror, battles of Algiers.
And they speak to me in English
and I say Lucknow, Arbenz. I say indigo,

Hiroshima, continents soaked in tea.
I play the drumbeat of stamps. I invoke
Mrs. Cummings, U.S. consul in Athens,
I say Ishi, Custer, Wounded Knee.
And Cairo's taxi drivers tell me
your Arabic is unbelievably good.
Tell the truth now, tell the truth,
how long have you been with us?
I say my first name is little lion,
my last name is broken branch.
I sing "Happiness uncontainable"
and "field greeting in March"
until I'm sad and tired of truth,
and as usual I'm never believed.
Then they lead me through congestion,
gritty air, narrow streets crowded with
Pepsi and Daewoo and the sunken faces
of the poor. And when we arrive, Cairo's
taxi drivers and I speak all the languages
of the world, and we argue and argue about
corruption, disillusionment, the missed chances,
the wicked binds, the cataclysmic fares.

Letter from Lynchburg

I write you from a small college in Virginia, where I was invited to teach a course on writing poetry. The college is in a small city with a convoluted history of golden ages and periods of slowness and recession, all depending on influential outsiders and the changes they brought with them. Like many small cities, it is mercilessly at the whim of a bigger world. The city's name, evoking Billie Holiday's strange fruit, is like a bad pun no southern city would envy. In fact, the story of the name is older than the phenomenon of lynching and bespeaks a gentler disposition; it refers to a Quaker, who resorted to the ferry business because he was opposed to slavery on religious grounds. Lynch was also opposed to slavery for personal reasons. His father, Charles, had arrived here as an indentured servant held in a long, humiliating bondage. The ferry turned out to be the real catalyst for the town's development and growth. And the lessons are in some ways clear: Some lives choose to depend on oppressing others; other lives thrive by reaching out. Luckily, and I believe this is always true in the end, those who reach out prevail. The story also affirms what I learned in my economics classes. Cities are built where "man" has to change his means of transport, at the spot where he has to get off his horse and walk, or swim or float or sail. And herein lies the paradox that cities and individual lives share: we settle where we are supposed to cross, spend lifetimes where we were supposed to stay only a short while.

Before the Civil War and after, Lynchburg was considered one of the richest towns in the country, a center for initial gathering of tobacco, where at the beginning of summer, farmers sailed their flat boats on the James River. At the docks, slaves emptied those boats, placing the pales in huge cylindrical containers called "hogsheads" and rolled them to warehouses built from the wood of virgin forests, where the tobacco was auctioned and shipped to buyers all over the planet. In those hot, humid days, fragrances mixed, the fresh cut tobacco, the wood, the river and the sweat of masters and slaves. These reminders of the city's history clung to it long after the slaves were freed and their descendants founded their neighborhood on the remains of rich merchants' homes, long after they left the town altogether heading north, as the South began a slumber that can still be detected on the faces of the region where I lived for twelve of my twenty American years.

The students in the class I teach here, by the sheer looks of their faces, point to the history of this city and its past. The young man with the long hair carries in his strands not only the history of the hippies' recent commotion, but the history of the pioneers, Davie Crockett and his fur cap, the white settlers who lived in the woods learning the Indians' hunting ways and hunting down Indians. The pioneer who disliked slaves and masters, who loved fresh air, and feared God only because he feared the dark. Another student, polite, and quiet. Her face evokes the heritage of rich, southern families, merchants of cotton and tobacco who longed for aristocratic ways. She is shy, this young woman, and her future worries me. Another quiet young woman, her Mediterranean features suggest another history that began when the city shifted to industry with the cigarette makers of Green Slave, Ruby, My Sweet Heart, and Spanish Queen, the iron foundries that smelted the ore from nearby mines, the shoe factories that employed a third of the population, B & W makers of the doomed nuclear reactor at Three Mile Island, and General Electric who could afford to come and leave because of low wages and weak labor unions. I see in her face the distance she has crossed alone away from her grandparents and their old world and settled identities. And there is the smiling young woman, her round face with its green eyes of the China Sea. An Amerasian, she is another history that is still with us. American imperialism abroad, the technology plants here, cell phones, and computer networking systems. New families with Northern and Midwestern accents, and twangs, inflection, and timbres from languages across the globe. New knowledges, and houses of compressed wood built and torn in no time at all.

I enter the classroom, and I see a map of the Middle East drawn to depict the political geography of the Old Testament. There is Madian, the Gulf of Ilat, Judea, Samaria, Canaan and the Sea of Galilee, ancient names of extinct cities now evoked to strip hundreds of villages of their Arab names. There's the Nile and its delta, before Alexander, before my countryman Callimachus, before Cairo, the city I love most. Patches of empty land full of the graves of ancient prophets, and the dead of recent wars.

Between the histories of my students and the history drawn on the map, my heart, imagination and my thoughts linger. Both are far from me. Yet I live with both, no matter how the present itself seems distant. The class begins and we introduce ourselves. It is amazing how small we see ourselves, how disjointed and alone. What binds me to these people, I ask myself. The news of their economy, their politics, their festive moments and sadnesses seem far from me. How many cities have I lived in where I never read the local newspaper, never knew the name of the mayor, never knew what made a mass of people coexist, and even grow to admire or detest each other. One city after another, one morning after another, coffee cup after coffee cup. What I know about a place no longer has the curiosity of the tourist, or the traveler. My knowledge of cities is a way to read the landscape and the faces and to tie the future with an element of sequence and consequence. I read the history and the present of this land in the same way I read a map—so that I do not get lost.

But we are now in class talking about poetry as if poetry is capable of filling the historical, political, social and psychological gaps between us. The truth of the matter is I distrust anyone who says poetry can always gather us, and I distrust anyone who says it can't. In the end, I believe in the importance of the attempt, its necessity. And I believe the poetry is in the attempt.

In the now empty and decaying tobacco warehouses here in Lynchburg, who knows and who remembers those who visited here and those who died here? The history of the city, as presented by its historians, begins with this sentence: "First came the buffalo, and the elk and otter. Then came the Monacan Indians." None of them remains. But we have reminders, some of them painful. Across my window, a security guard paces, small clouds of cigarette smoke blowing from his mouth. He is a reincarnation of a soldier long ago, a rifle strapped to his shoulder, pacing the tobacco warehouses after they were turned into munitions stores during the Civil War. And the African women on the TV news beating their wash on stones may as well be descendants of the slave women by the James River who beat their masters' wash on stones just a few miles from here.

And what can bridge these gaps other than poetry? Those moments exist in our phrases as we form our thoughts. The faces I describe to you, and the lives I conjure, live in our poetic imagination. They live in the words I now send your way. Poetry tells us, without reminders there is no future. This is what makes poetry capable of shaping the ideals for what we want to be as people and what we want the world to be. It is the removal of a pain that has occurred or a pain we are afraid will occur. It is saying what we know and retrieving what we forgot, or discovering a new knowledge that was not there before we looked for it.

My writing in English, a language I adopted, and my involvement in translating Arabic poetry, brings this home to me repeatedly. The language I possess is tenuous and fragile, and the reader is, at best, curious. It is not worth trying to please any one. What will stand out, and what will ultimately satisfy, is the honest effort, the poem that sends its author to the library, the one that makes its writer curious and even slightly amazed. Here, the mind follows a phrase, an idea, coaxes it, interrogates it, until it leads to a new map, until it reaches the truth of its meaning.

Poetry as living and living as poetry are then this rigorous attempt to understand the world, present, past, and future, and to understand the self in the world, in its maturity and youth, in its solitude, and in its interaction with others. The self facing the mountain, the self and the ceaseless ebb of time. Tell me what you know truthfully, and I tell you what I know truthfully. In any language, at any time, any place. The thought in the feeling. The truth in the song.

Echo & Elixir

Maybe love is a walk to astonishment.
Or a ship stranded on the shore of oblivion.
The infinity in the atom,
the treasures found in a word from long ago
now retrieved,
and the mind's chamber so luminous
it sees nothing but you.
Soul of my heart and my eyes' lanterns.
My loved one's hair is tangled
like a tumbleweed, soft as down.
My gazelle and the music in her walk.
My freckled wonder. My apricot.
Maybe these are the heart's cymbals that guide its trance:
Rouhi. Hayati, Nour Ayami.
Maybe to say "I love you" in another language
is not to love you at all.
Hear me say it, *Habibti.*
I say: *N'hibik*

On the Road with Adonis

On an eight-lane stretch of highway, with traffic alongside us streaming at about seventy miles an hour, Adonis looked around and ahead, then said: "When the oil goes, all of this will be gone." It was one of many memorable moments with the visionary poet. The image haunts me sometimes when I drive the wide highways of Southeast Michigan, months after the poet's visit, during which we also travelled to other parts of the United States.

Adonis's poetry, early and late, is full of powerful, often violent visions, though one cannot say that he necessarily projects a dark vision of humanity. The poet is simply alert, he has powerful faculties and he must let them speak to him, unimpacted by the dissonance of others' views or any consensus of opinion. Among the many joys of being on the road with Adonis last year was being in the company of such a lively mind whose awareness triggers not only responses but also responsibilities.

Over the decades, Adonis must have trained his senses to look for what surprises, what others tend to ignore. This may be why his images and metaphors are so startling and unique in the mode of a sculptor who takes a hunch and builds on it with great care and thought.

In his social interactions, Adonis seems to feel that what people think and observe can be an extension of his faculties. Many times I saw him engrossed in head-to-head conversations with young poets and writers. The subjects varied, and Adonis did little talking as his interlocutor relayed what he knew. At one gathering, I watched Adonis listen patiently as a throng of Arab professionals, like a classroom of young overachievers, tried to impress him with their knowledge of Arab poetry and culture. They went on like this for at least two hours until they were tired out. Once Adonis noticed they had finished, he began a wonderful discourse about his childhood in Qassabin and his university years in Damascus. He spoke in vivid detail about the people who helped him reach Shukri al-Qawatli, Syria's president, who was so impressed with the young poet that he offered him a scholarship. He spoke about his interaction with Georges Saadeh, head of the Syrian Nationalist Party, who was very supportive of him as a university student and party recruit.

From personal memories, the talk widened to encompass facets of Arab culture, where clearly Adonis had no rival. Adonis's criticism of the oppressive role of religion was unsparing. A woman in the group became incensed and was visibly made uncomfortable both by what the poet was saying and her inability to refute it even as he welcomed her interruptions.

On that evening and on other occasions he has spoken to audiences, Adonis shocked his listeners and also made them nod with approval. People simply could not stop listening to him. He was fully himself, impeccably gracious and considerate, but willing to shred any inconsistencies presented to him.

Heated dialogues are ordinary happenings in Adonis's life as a public intellectual. I am sure he finds them wearying, though he genuinely craves dialogue. Once, as I described an event to him, he replied: "Are we just going to read poetry to these people?" Perhaps readings do wear him out, for in truth only a conceited poet thinks that people are dying to hear him.

Of course, people lined up to see Adonis, to speak to him, to have him sign his books. The part he enjoyed most was the dialogue. He craves new conversations, new poetry, and new art. He commented on beautiful faces, paintings, clothes, and even cowboy boots. Instinct and experience have taught him to dismiss many of the pretenses to newness he hears of. But he's always on the lookout and latches on to any idea that inspires him.

Among the many notions Adonis undermines is the stereotype of the poet as a spaced-out, romantic figure lost in the fog of his imagination. A lover of wine, he is enhanced and slightly more buoyant when we shared a glass but no less focused. He does not drop projects or appointments; Adonis is always on time. He organizes years in advance and remembers exactly what he has promised. Practical and useful as such attentiveness is, it began to seem to me a kind of philosophy, even a kind of politics where respect for one's time and commitments broadens to a respect for other humans, the short spans of their existence, and the earth they inhabit.

It was perhaps fitting then that after I had translated Adonis's poetry, he and I would take to the road to expand what had been a lyrical friendship into some epic territories. A series of fond memories stand out, such as the many long and wonderfully joyous conversations Adonis had with my three-year old daughter. But more importantly, I believe I was given some access to a way of mapping time and to a kind of poetics, too, in which art negotiates aspirations and reality, and where the body is always at the cusp of an idea. For that, no thanks are ever sufficient, especially as the gift is bound to radiate for as long as I live.

Skyping with Saadi, Channeling Li Po

Every now and then, I have the chance to chat with the great Iraqi poet Saadi Youssef. We exchange news, talk poetry and more often than not commiserate on the bad shape of our homelands. Also, while Saadi is speaking, I often find myself listening to an unwritten chapter of modern Arabic poetry, as if a time portal has opened up to a wondrous and intriguing past I knew nothing of. This time, I skyped with Saadi to query him about lines in poems of his that I was translating. When we were finished, I asked him what he was working on.

To be sure, Saadi is always writing poems, sometimes several poems a day. But he's also always working on something else, perhaps assembling a new diwan (book of poems) from among his most recent poems. This time, he told me he's translating the great Chinese poet Li Po (702–62 AD), also known as Li Bai.

I was very fascinated. I teach Li Po in a comparative poetics class at the University of Michigan. In fact, it was Li Po who led me to discover earlier Chinese texts such as the *Book of Songs* (Shi Jing) and the *Songs of the South* (Chu Si), both are works of astounding beauty.

Saadi asked me if I'm familiar with "The River Merchant's Wife," Ezra Pound's translation of a poem by Li Po. I said I knew the poem and the story of how Pound stumbled upon Japanese versions of Chinese poetic masterpieces among the notebooks of the Japanese scholar Ernest Fenollosa (1853–1908). From these translations, Pound published the Cathay poems in 1915. The volume includes "River Merchant's Wife," but is attributed to Rihaku not to Li Po—Rihaku being Li Po's Japanese name.

As we talked, I looked up the Cathay poems. Pound, as it turned out, titled the book *Cathay, Translations by Ezra Pound: For the Most Part from the Chinese of Rihaku, from the Notes of the late Ernest Fenollosa, and the Decipherings of the Professors Mori and Ariga.* Nonetheless, the poems were attributed to Pound as their author, and remain so today. "River Merchant's Wife" is one of the most anthologized poems in the English language and is always included among Pound's compositions. In college, I encountered the poem as belonging to Ezra Pound, no questions asked.

Saadi then told me that was the impression the great Iraqi poet Badr Shakir Al-Sayyab (1926–64) had when he translated "The River Merchant's Wife." Al-Sayyab included it in *Qasa'id mukhtara min al-shi'r al-'alami al-hadith* (A Selection of International Modern Poems), an anthology he published in 1955. According to Saadi, Al-Sayyab's translation of the poem, which I have not been able to locate, was in metrical Arabic verse, or *tafai'la*, the new poetic form that he and the other great Iraqi poet of the period, Nazik Al-Malaika, had pioneered.

Li Po's "A River Merchant's Wife" in Sayyab's resonant Arabic based on Pound's English verse is doubtlessly a remarkable poem emblematic of Modern poetry in the twentieth century, where translation played an essential role in freeing languages all over the world and the poets working in them from inherited conventions that seemed to stifle creativity. Pound felt this need to bust loose from the prosody and diction of English poetry written in the late nineteenth century that was choking his voice, as did other writers at the time. Modernist critic Hugh Kenner reports that in 1912, Pound visited Ford Maddox Ford, a writer Pound greatly admired, and showed him his poems. Ford reacted by rolling on the floor in mock agony in response to Pound's overwrought poetic language. It is no secret that Pound's discovery of Asian poetry, and his translations of Chinese, freed him tremendously and gave him a sense of lyricism he would not have discovered otherwise. Plenty of evidence also shows that T. S. Eliot benefited from translation. Translating French Symbolist poets helped him adhere to Pound's advice to seek poetic beauty by composing "in the sequence of the musical phrase, not in sequence of a metronome."

As such, Li Po's "A River Merchant's Wife," as it reached young Saadi Youssef in 1955 (via Sayyab via Pound), was a powerful poetic cocktail that mixed Chinese classicism with Anglophone and Arabic modernist poetics. And complicated as the poem's genealogy may have been, it was doubtlessly a seamless lyric due to its clear images and its understated expressions of emotion. Saadi went on to say that "Risalah min zawjat tajer al-nahr" (A Letter from the River Merchant's Wife), attributed to Ezra Pound, inspired him in 1956 to write a poem of his own, titled "Ilhah" (Insistence).

I knew "Insistence" quite well as I myself translated it sometime in the late 1990s. In "Insistence," Saadi offers the persona of a young river merchant who is filled with longing for his wife, matching that of Li Po's female speaker. Saadi's poet speaker implores the captain, Salim Marzouq, to take him on his ship:

> Salim Marzouq, take me   on a ship
> on a ship. Take my eyes for ransom . . . I'll do what you wish
> except what women are supposed to.
> Salim Marzouq   my sad wife
> is a prisoner in her father's house
> in a village near Sihan, arid without palms.

Saadi takes the Modernist appropriation of Li Po to its logical conclusion. He localizes the tender feelings of Li Po's female speaker and responds to them with a local male voice rising from the marshlands of Basra.

Decades after writing "Insistence," Saadi discovered that the poem that inspired him to write "Insistence" and other poems of the period actually belonged to Li Po, not Ezra Pound. And now, six decades after "Insistence," Saadi was full on working on a translation of poems by the great master Li Po, based on English translation. "Li Po's poetry is rooted in modern poetry, even in Arabic poetry," he explained. Indeed! And when I said earlier that Saadi is always working on something, this time it delights me to no end to see one of the masters of modern Arabic poetry renewing his voice by rediscovering his complicated poetic roots.

Saadi's new poems echo this intricately braided inheritance, intersecting his subtle voice with Li Po's acute sensitivity to nature. We also have the solace of drink, the pangs of solitude and the self-deprecating tone that made Li Po's poetry so endearing and moving, and so modern. But unlike Li Po, who tends to ease us off his painful moments at the end of his poems, Saadi sometimes works his imagistic impressions into intense dramatic conclusions as in the poems "Woodpecker" and "Morning Scene."

Imagining Saadi as the Li Po of our modern times, I see his poems as combinations of brush strokes that dip inward into emotion and outward into nature, and from this intense exchange of image and disclosure emerges poignant renderings of an extraordinary inner life, rich in empathy and resonant with transcendence.

Poems and Days

(A Reader's Memoir)

A tranquilizing spirit presses now
On my corporeal frame, so wide appears
The vacancy between me and those days,
Which yet have such self-presence in my mind
That sometimes when I think of them I seem
Two consciousnesses-conscious of myself,
And of some other being.
—William Wordsworth, "The Two-Part Prelude" (II, 27–33)

The question is whether, if we venture ourselves a second time with Vanity Fair, the Copperfields, the Richardsons, we shall be able to find some other form of pleasure to the place of that careless rapture which floated us along so triumphantly in the first instance.
—Virginia Woolf, "On Re-reading Novels"

It feels as though I knew this book by heart and that I took in so many details that re-reading it was simply a matter of checking that they were still in their proper places . . . the words were where they should be, and the books told a story you could follow; you could re-read, and, on re-reading, re-encounter, enhanced by the certainty that you would encounter those words again, the impression you had felt the first time. This pleasure has never ceased for me; I do not read much, but I have never stopped re-reading . . . I re-read the books I love and I love the books I re-read, and each time it is the same enjoyment, whether I re-read twenty pages, three chapters, or the whole book: an enjoyment of complicity, of collusion, or more especially, and in addition, of having in the end found kin again.
—George Perec, *W or the Memory of Childhood*

Perhaps what we get from a poem is an impression that seeds itself in memory and mind, a sort of legend that grows even as we read the work again. Also, a sense of wonder and admiration, caught in the impression we've made of the poet, or something akin to love grows to become unconditional until we do not know why it is we've loved this poet or poem.

In writing this essay/memoir, I meant mainly to recapture the wonder and amazement I had of poems I read in my first years of writing. Returning to them, however, I found that while the precise dates and places were not difficult to recall, the circumstances were blurry. I have never had to explain why I loved the poems, but in writing about them, I had to find the reasons. In some cases, the reasons were apparent. But when I tried to recall my impressions, I became uncertain whether these thoughts were in fact old. Reading what I wrote on the margin of the books and anthologies where I read the poems, many of these impressions felt like new discoveries that had never crossed my mind.

It could be just a matter of memory pretending to know what it had never experienced, and polishing old thoughts as shiny new goods. Whatever the case may be, these poems have continued to renew themselves to me or in me, and to use Perec's analogy of kin, my fresh responses to them are like the children of old friends whose bear such great resemblance to their parents that I cannot help but extend them the same affection. And having again the same thoughts of them was like seeing old photographs of ancestors whose faces touch us with fondness. "What thou lov'st well is thy true heritage," writes Ezra Pound. I offer these new and old thoughts about these poems in the spirit of passing on treasured goods so that they be read and re-read, loved and forgotten and loved again.

Chattanooga, June 1987

> And Baghdad darken and the
> bridge . . .
> And through Arabia the edge
> "You, Andrew Marvell"
> Archibald MacLeish

MacLeish's is not the first poem I read in English. In my high school in Louisiana, I read William Carlos Williams's "Red Wheel Barrow" and it simply made no sense to me. The teacher and class went through it the way I remember we went through our inoculations in Libya, a brief, painful obligation. In college, in my first bona fide literature class, two lines in MacLeish's poem appealed to me: "And Baghdad darken and the bridge / Across the silent river gone." This was in the mid-1980s; Baghdad did not make the news much then, but it was a name that meant a great deal to me and here it was in an American poem. The passage goes on to Arabia where the "evening widen[s] and steal[s] on." The thrill of finding oneself recognized somehow was quite energizing. Now I wanted to know what the poem was actually saying. I would not know Marvell for a few years and what MacLeish was trying to tell him.

At the time, my college career had been like an air hockey puck, bouncing from one major to another. The intro to literature class where I read MacLeish's poem was like an oasis for a lost desert traveler, and that passage in the poem indicated to me that I could rest there. In my last year of high school, I'd become serious about religion, seeking a way to cement my identity. I'd finished high school in a boarding school in Louisiana without going home to Libya, where a group of my closest friends, all teenagers, were jailed en masse, accused of taking part in a plot to assassinate Col. Qaddafi. I could easily have been one of them. A stretch of exile lay before me, and without a sense of career or calling, I needed to decide who and what I was. At least that is what my high school principal/therapist, Brother Jeffery, told me. With patience and openness, he listened to my angst-filled monologues, and when telling him that I thought I wanted to be a good Muslim, he promptly told me, "Then that is what you must do."

But I was also puzzled by the question. How can one decide to be something? Aren't our selves already determined, haven't we been shaped already? Isn't "deciding" to be something a kind of fabrication? Being a Muslim was an easy answer and I had none better. It was impossible then to read the Quran for guidance. Greater conditioning was needed and also a community to interpret, reiterate, and reinforce. The holy book's music helped, and some people I met along the way offered examples of decency. But for years after taking the straight path, there was only the long flat stretch of time ahead and the blankness inside that nothing would fill. I felt this sadness when I sought community in my first year of college in Tennessee, where I attempted to study architecture, a community soon divided between Sunni and Shiite, while the TV churned hate and Reagan pulled imperialist wool over the citizenry's eyes. I felt I was being hit from all sides. God demanded so many aches, especially an estrangement from my own body and its instincts. Still, I ploughed on working on planning conferences, fundraising for a new mosque, writing for and editing a weekly newsletter, all the while feeling like I'm pushing against the current of my fellow believers. I knew we came from defeated societies, and we all needed the sweetness of faith to give us meaning; but it was impossible to keep facing the roving intolerance and rigidity, the sense of superiority that the faithful felt at all times, attitudes and states of mind that projected outward comfort among the believers, but that never settled in me.

I was failing in school, too. I changed majors, from architecture to business, and then from that to something else, barely keeping a passing average. Once I knew a course was beyond repair—a sure F—a guilty pleasure filled me. I could then stay home and read. I have a distinct memory of reading Alex Haley's *Autobiography of Malcolm X*, Muhammad Assad's *The Road to Mecca*, Ralph Ellison's *Invisible Man*, Dostoevsky's *Notes from the Underground*, Kafka's *Castle*, and a moving ethnography about poor families in Kentucky. All offered various engagements and prolonged spells of identification that widened my soul. At some point, I changed universities altogether to escape the distractions of Muslim activism, moved to a town where I knew no one. I was ready for poetry at last, and Baghdad and Arabia in MacLeish's poem were my first destinations.

Chattanooga, July 1987

> And by came an Angel who had a
> bright key,
> And he opened the coffins & set them
> all free;
> "The Chimney Sweeper"
> William Blake

Growing up in Libya, I never quite sensed the fatalism that surrounded me. People were not markedly religious, and even as practicing believers, the men in my family were driven by what I can only think of as a kind of Protestant work ethic. They built businesses and watched over them meticulously to succeed. Charity was at the center of that work ethic. There was always mention of *zakat*, the required annual alms worth 2.5 percent of one's wealth that had to be given to the needy, and *sadaqah*, which was optional.

My mother practiced her own kind of charity, mostly centered around food and clothing. Women came to assist her at home on certain chores such as fluffing the wool stuffed in mattresses, or washing the rugs, or making the annual patch of lamb jerky. They went home with their pay, a bag full of clothes, a sack of meat, and whatever our house garden could offer. More than once, she ransacked my wardrobe giving away favorite fashionable shirts or pants that I put away for special occasions and that she thought I did not need because I rarely wore them. Though living in a city, we were still the products of an egalitarian Bedouin society, where giving must not seem like charity, and receiving it is never a cause for solicitousness. Indeed, God provided each his *rizq* (fortune), but human intervention was the main method among the lord's mysterious ways.

I came to Blake's poem before reading Dickens, but with familiarity with Marx and Sayyed Qutb's and Ali Shariati's critiques of capitalism under my belt. These, in addition to the horror of a class-stratified society that my upbringing had instilled in me, along with disgust while hearing the triumphant Republican rhetoric of the 1980s, made Blake's poem a revelation. The poem explained systems of cruelty and deception, running alongside their opposites, kindness and innocence. Blake lines up the moral conflict in a strong contrast—Religion (Christianity) + the upper classes versus the poor—but the presentation is quite complex. We enter innocence from the inside, where no light of doubt or skepticism enters. The speaker of the poem is an older boy, who supposedly knows more than Little Tom Dacre, the new boy whose father had sold into the slave labor of chimney sweeping. The speaker assures Tom that all will be all right. That same night, Tom's subconscious mind regurgitates in dream the religious rationalization of his disposability. The dream is the third dark layer of innocence we encounter in the poem. Upon telling it to the other boys, all are reassured that "if all do their duty, they need not fear harm" and go on about their deadly jobs. Among the villains in the poem is the Angel holding the bright key, promising the chimney sweepers heavenly reward, and God, who only allows the boys to come close to him after they die of chimney sweeping.

Discussing this poem with fellow students in the class where I encountered it, it was difficult to convince them that Blake was offering a horrific version of how religion was indeed an opiate of the masses. Seeing myself then as a Muslim with a progressive notion of social justice, I felt stymied by the conservatism of my fellow students. This was in Chattanooga, Tennessee, where these students found it difficult to penetrate Blake's layers of dramatic irony. "The boy will die happily," someone argued. "The boy is using his imagination to overcome a difficult situation," another stated. Or worse yet, "The boy has a positive outlook." Even the casually religious refused to see God and religion in the harsh light that Blake sheds on them and refused to see what chimney sweeping involved. I felt frustrated by that encounter but also that I found an ally in Blake, a sort of artist prophet that I could return to for succor.

Blake's allure remained with me; his paintings and the depth and ambition of his cultural project were indeed radical. His poems, not just the innocence and experience project, are studies in contrastive light—a Romantic esthetic of high and low, ecstasy and despair, reunion and separation. In many ways, he reminded me of Halaj and Ibn Arabi, the great Arab mystical poets who held on tenaciously to the light of their poetic visions. I admired, too, that Blake seemed to have the artistry under control, that he lived a full life and a somewhat normal one But it seemed also that his constancy in the midst of a tumultuous vision was also fueled by madness. His light burned you or froze you or cut you; it did not quite embrace. He would come to mind often as an ideal and a lighthouse. I thought of him again on my first visit to Cairo, a city not unlike his London, where children Tom Dacre's age sold jasmine sprigs and begged and when spoken too gave a version of life not different from what we encounter in "The Chimney Sweeper." In later conversations with perfectly reasonable relatives in Libya, I would hear of fate as an explanation of all sorts of harm. A needless death is explained with the phrase "his time has come." Idiotic risks and deaths caused by outright negligence are justified by fatalistic explanations of God's will. Not knowing it and realizing the futility of challenging such beliefs, I found myself edging away from social encounters at home, unable to sit through funeral wakes or to commiserate with the ill or the injured, hearing that loss and affliction can so easily be explained away with the balm of religious sentiment. I walked away from the darkness with Blake's poem like a flashlight in my hand.

Chattanooga, May 1988

> you must live with great seriousness
> like a squirrel, for example.
> "On Living"
> Nazim Hikmet
> Tr. Randy Blasing and Mutlu Konuk

With Hikmet, memory is certainly playing a game with me. I know that I read the poems in a book with the poet's photo on the cover borrowed from the Chattanooga Public Library, but I was a university student at the time and I'm sure the book would have been there. I know for sure that I held the book with both hands like a prize when I found it. Poems such as "On Living" and "Biography" resounded with heroic ardor, and though a familiar communist timbre chimed in, it was the humanist who won out in the end. After reading "Things I Did Not Know I Loves," I turned to the face on the cover to make the impressions sink in. Hikmet wrote "On Living" when he was sixty and while suffering from angina. Clearly, he knew that his life as a poet had reached a certain fullness, but he seemed aware, after decades in jail, that freedom in exile was a kind of standstill. The Cold War was on full throttle when his photo was taken, Turkey far from a proletariat revolution, the Soviets comfortable with the status quo. That's what the face added to the poems.

One must live seriously, Hikmet says in "On Living," so much so "that you can die for people." And you are willing to die, because you don't believe death, or in it, and that life will continue, though it may not be your own life. It's a great inspiring message, and an ingenuous idea that honors sacrifice, while it somehow assures us of some sort of eternal life. A few months prior to visiting the library to borrow Hikmet's poems, I had an important discovery. One afternoon, as I was about to perform my daily prayer something became clear in my mind. For weeks my body performed the motions, uttered the words, but the soul was elsewhere, despondent and adrift. I'd been fasting on that day too, but there was no union there. I'd relied on hunger in the past to turn me inside out of such feelings of loss, and through faith and communion assure me that my life mattered. But not that afternoon. I could not will that sense of belonging that had sustained me through much solitude. I sought words that mattered to me: "And if all the trees in the earth were pens, and if the sea, with seven more seas to help it, were ink, the words of God could not be exhausted," I read in the Luqman chapter in the Quran. What other words of God are there to be written and who was going to say them or write them? Hikmet's poem struck me as belonging to those new words taken down from the same sea.

Through Hikmet I developed an excitement about language, an awareness of the barriers that sound and sense could break for us. Hikmet's face, looking like that of my kin and sounding the prayers I wanted to chant, released me to myself. I should also say that Randy Blasing and Mutlu Konuk's translation convinced me of the power of translation. Every time anyone started complaining about what is lost in translation, I wanted to recite a Hikmet poem in English to disabuse him or her of that notion. Perhaps God had translation in mind when he spoke of his words requiring all the world's seas and trees to write them.

Chattanooga, August 1988

> It so happens I'm tired of being a man.
> "Walking Around"
> Pablo Neruda
> Tr. Robert Bly

What a startling poem Neruda's "Walking Around" was and remains. A poem that makes you sit up reading, exhilarating and profoundly sad at the same time. The poem startled at every turn with its surrealism and exotic setting. It comes from *Residencia en la Terra*, a book of poems Neruda wrote while he served as a consular officer for Chile in Sri Lanka. He'd served for two years in Burma by then and would go on to work in Asia for a few more. What did it mean for him to be from Chile and a poet from Chile at the time? How much explaining did he have to do about his country and his profession? What sort of business did he have to conduct between Colombo and Santiago?

I'd not read "Walking Around" on its own. The poem, like a lead singer who'd left his band to fend for itself, has had a very successful solo career. But in truth, the poems of *Residencia en la Terra* together offered a daring way of seeing the world. Here are some startling images that expressed to me a new sense of the world's physicality:

Coffins under sail . . .
and pensive young girls married to notary publics . . .
caskets sailing up the vertical river of the dead . . .
the needle of death looking for a thread

and the beds go sailing toward a port
where death is waiting dressed like an admiral . . .

These dreamy images happen to have sailing as a motif, perhaps an expression of Neruda's long maritime journey to reach his post in Asia. All arrivals are disappointing; the young girls landing in the arms of notary publics are contractually trapped in a kind of death. One could not think of a less romantic outcome. And what awful things will the needle of death do once it finds its thread? The image of death dressed like an admiral is slightly comical. Neruda in these poems writhes from the absurdity of life.

Lonely and feeling desolate, the poet in "Gentlemen Without Company" walks a fertile sexual landscape that mocks him. He begins to believe that others are conspiring against him "dressed in sleeping costumes / and give each other as passwords of profound kisses." They deride the poet's loneliness by making love on the beach as he walks by. Then he notices "women's breasts sparkling like eyes." Here the voyeur is being gazed at and rendered powerless by his longing. The entangled lovers become "an immense forest . . . with huge flowers like mouths and rows of teeth" threatening to consume him.

In "Walking Around," Neruda renders his alienation in kinetic terms. Feeling "dried up, water proof, like a swan made of felt," he simply asks us to believe him. The smell of barbershops makes the poet sob. There's both clarity and ambiguity here. A mix of talc, the wooly smell of hair, oil and citron scented aftershaves, the scent of sharp cleanliness and the warm essence of human skin, all reminders of grooming and intimacy. The image brought me memories of the antiquated barbershops of my own childhood when, during moments of silence, the sound of the blade shaving a scalp was natural like a cricket's chirp and also otherworldly. But the poet keeps the reasons for his fit of sobbing to himself. He demands that we trust him.

Mention of the barbershop elicits other corporeal images. The streets are "hideous like cracks in the skin." This image precedes two contrasting moments: "hospitals where bones fly out the window" and "false teeth forgotten in coffee pot." The first belongs to Baudelaire, violent and sadistic. The second could also be Baudelairian, but it suggests another side to the world the poet is describing; it's a world of neglect. Anything can happen in this world, and the poet too is bound to feel that his body is morphing into a form of objectified life. I've always had some doubts about the last image of the poem, where "slow dirty tears are falling" off the laundry. It's no match to the poem's opening line. But the sentimentality of the tears is unsettled by a mention of "orthopedic shops," which startles us. What remains wonderful and inspiring about Neruda, especially in this group of poems, is the freedom and limberness of his imagination, how often and willingly we go with him wherever his poems want to take us.

Chattanooga, October 1988

> to help the killer kill—a terrible
> thing—
> and I would like to be kind to my
> self
> in everything
>
> Cesar Vallejo
> tr. Clayton Eshleman and Jose Barcia

The poem quoted above begins with the line, "For several days, I have felt an exuberant, political need / to love, to kiss affection on its two cheeks." The exuberance is multifaceted; it is passionate and deeply responsive to anyone ("whoever hid in his wrath, / whoever sweats, whoever passes, whoever shakes his person in my soul"). It is also playful and tender and democratic, teasing and helpful. The poet wants to be "useful" and wants "to help the good one become a little bit bad . . ." The exuberance comes to the poet when he feels sad or "when happiness hurts me," and its source is love:

> this one, my own, this one, the world's,
> Interhuman and parochial, maturely aged!
> It comes, perfectly timid,
> From the foundation, from the public groin,
> and, coming from afar,

The love is the poet's and the world's. This is a conflation that Vallejo never quite resolves. It's also a crossbred feeling that comes out of habit, or a savored, well-crafted thing. It's all of these combined, arising from the seat of our reproductive instinct, or from an otherworldly distance. The poet wants it badly and revels in its domination of his state of mind.

Vallejo's playfulness is half Apollinaire, half Baudelaire. He wants to kiss "whoever gives me what I forgot in my breast, / on his Dante, on his Chaplin," whoever moves him, resurrecting in him what he had hid deep inside him, his art, high or low. Most astoundingly, the poem ends with the poet wishing "to help the killer kill—a terrible thing— / and I would like to be kind to my self / in everything." The poet pushes the feeling to its logical and devastating end, beyond conscience in search of radical empathy. He wants to assist by being inside others, their passions, their weaknesses and their terrible deeds. Vallejo, in that sense, is a poet of fire, consuming and willing to be consumed by the "interhuman," driven by the strength of his vulnerability.

In the poem "The Black Riders," where Vallejo shows himself to be a scholar of suffering, he writes, "There are blows in life so violent—I can't answer / Blows as if from the hatred of God." The suffering occurs repeatedly, and the form of the poem resembling a villanelle with its refrain offers a promissory note that the poet must deliver on. Vallejo loves to argue, and he is full of evidence to assert his truth. Similarly, in "I Am Going to Talk about Hope," the poet feels pain and denies that it is his alone. "I do not feel this suffering as Cesar Vallejo. I am not suffering now as a creative person, or as a man, nor even as a simple living being," he writes. The poet's pain is so prevalent and powerful, he'd feel if he were not alive. He wonders about its cause and finds it has none. He compares it to others' pain and it pales in comparison. Still, he has this pain that does not waver, and what he feels belongs to everyone, giving new meaning to Whitman's "For every atom belonging to me as good belongs to you."

This empathy has a devastating side to it, for life seems to be a matter of chance, and we are in some ways replaceable.

> Every bone in me belongs to others;
> and I may have robbed them.
> I came to take something for myself that maybe
> was meant for some other man;
> and I start thinking that, if I had not been born,
> another poor man could have drunk this coffee . . .

The first line here rephrases Whitman's verb "belong" again. Every bone of his body is not merely as good as belonging to others; it actually belongs to them. The identification with others here leads to a sense of the absurd. Vallejo can only find a shared misery, a uniform and unshakable misfortune. This invariably brings on a confrontation with fate and God, who is ignorant of human suffering. Only such knowledge could make Him divine again. He writes:

> My God, if you have been man,
> today you would know how to be God
> but you always lived so well,
> that now you feel nothing of your own creation.
> And the man who suffers you: he is God!

Vallejo alleviates human suffering to the divine because the human alone understands the nature of existence. In another poem, Vallejo humanizes God, who is tired and deserves our sympathy for he is worn out "like those who care for the sick . . ." and "he whispers with sweet contempt like a lover's." God is so fatigued that he begins to weep, and this fills the speaker with tenderness and love. He turns to God saying,

> I consecrate you, God, because you love so much;
> because you never smile; because your heart
> must all the time give you great pain . . .

And that is as it should be, because consecration is what Vallejo has been doing all along to everyone, so why not God?

Whether in this early poem or in the late poem I began with, consecration is Vallejo's business, and it comes from a reservoir of humanity deeper than anything we can encounter elsewhere in literature. What made Vallejo remarkable for me when I first read him, and what makes him deeply convincing now, is that the world and its suffering did not deceive him. Ecstasy was second nature to him, not only because he could step outside himself but also because he had a heart that took in the world, where the poet sometimes felt himself multiplied, overjoyed, and estranged.

Chattanooga, February 1989

> I give you back 1948.
> I give you all the years from then
>   Philip Levine
>   "You Can Have It"

At first, Levine's poetry resonated with me for its obvious alienation. He pointed to the angst that prosperity could not erase and the superficiality that a reluctant immigrant like myself can see through. His passion for others and his anger about the damage being caused to others was warmly familiar. Verbal irony here and there, and some cosmic irony along the way, for toughness' sake, but it was rage he wanted to get to. The poet refuses to accept tragedy and persists in his claim to grieve with passion even as he recognizes his condition as ordinary. I was reminded of a feeling I had watching Arthur Miller's and Shakespeare's tragedies and how I was unable to accept how dramatic irony bulldozed the play onward to its logical end due to the hero's "tragic flaw." I could not accept that a character could be so isolated that he would be left alone to deal with his shortcomings. Malik bin Nabi, the Algerian cultural critic once noted that tragedy is unacceptable to an Arab Muslim imagination, which rang true with me. Levine's rage at injustice struck that same nerve to me. There's no victim whose victimization can be redeemed by turning it into legend. God, or man, has to provide justice or recompense—replacing Isaac or Ishmael with the ram, for example. Otherwise, the human soul has to cry out the injustice and protest and remember.

Levine was the first poet I knew who made lyric out of work. I'd encountered critiques of industrialization in political science and economics, in novels and popular/folk protest songs, but here it was owned and sung. The figure of the brother in the poem "You Can Have It" is potentially the speaker himself, for he and his brother "are only one man," even as they work different jobs. The image of the year and its months and days falling "off the old newspapers/calendars, doctors' appointments, bonds,/wedding certificates, drivers licenses" is quite effective. I remember workshopping a poem with him once and he insisted on details like these. The newspapers and calendars are familiar images of time, he explained. "You have to push the image further until you come up with something that no one had thought of," he said. Originality is a higher degree of labor, he convinced me. In "You Can Have It," I did not care for the poet's plea that he be given back the moon, but the image of the brother with his "wide shoulders and a curse/for God" was appealing to me and remains so. If God does not provide the ram to save Ismail, let him be cursed.

Another dimension that opened Levine's poetry to me was his performances. I was lucky to watch him read his poems early on. The improvised, however practiced, storytelling with humor and self-deprecation thrown in worked beautifully with the poignant sad poems, which often had a twist of the knife at the end. After reciting a poem, Levine managed to lift the listeners from the deep sorrow into which his poems sank them. One's emotions fell and rose as the reading progressed, and he never undermined the pain addressed in his poem nor did he feel he needed to supplement it. The impact and the soothing relief were in waves; and the whole experience was quite cathartic. Levine's interviews, in print or on video, provided great testimonies of his passion and sly humor.

But it's his lyricism that keeps me returning to him. In poems such as "The Cemetery at Academy in California," Levine begins with a scene that combines humor and gravity. After napping in the cemetery, he finds that his boys had found their way to the outhouses and were spreading toilet paper all around. Comically contrite, the children gird themselves up as they pass a family visiting a loved one's grave. Like the Arab poet who has to be shown the wounds of love on him to earn a place of poetry, Levine here shows that he is flawed and perhaps unworthy of the gravity of his subject matter. This is done subtly and naturally and gives him credibility to proceed.

Levine thrusts imagery forward and deflects attention from the poet, carrying us along into the narrative with perfect emotional pitch. The poet appears still uncertain as to with whom to side, even when his "I" is involved in the drama. With great attention, he renders a stranger into our midst—the girl whose story the poem tells—and creates a powerful bond of identification.

Having become "a stranger to nothing" as he says at the end of the poem, Levine's portraits reveal sides of ourselves we are not likely to encounter anywhere else.

Chattanooga, May 1989

> from the other dancing—in Poland
> and Germany—
> oh God of mercy, oh wild God.
> "The Dancing"
> Gerald Stern

Stern s work immediately struck me with its dynamism and exuberance, how the poems could turn on a dime. Reading him, I thought of the plays of Eugene Ionesco, where horror and joy often overlap and where madness and peace are one and the same. Poetry in Stern's practice provides a chance to lose the self, to unleash its curiosity, the energy of the id foraging manically for joy. Stern's speaker often bumps into things, and the physical world becomes anthropomorphic in response. He can talk to a squirrel or sing to it; he could fight with the furniture in the room. We're also aware, as in the poem quoted above, that a plunge in melancholy can fall upon us, or we can fall into it after the poem's ecstatic flight, at any time. Stern's poetic genius lies in that fearlessness. In every encounter with the page, he calls to the imagination for a spiritual lift to where memory and dream contend for the inner eye.

Stern's work came as a graduation gift from my teacher Richard Jackson. I read it and returned to it often. When Jackson told me that Stern was coming to Chattanooga a year later, I drove 400 miles to get to meet him. For one afternoon, he was given to me to drive around town. A master storyteller, Stern would not stop talking. He spoke of the "evil Melons" of his native Pittsburgh mentioned in the poem quoted above. He told me of the assassination attempt on the brutal robber baron Henry Clay Frick with unforgettable drama. Enacting the whole episode, with his hand on his wounded neck like Frick, Stern rose to subdue the assassin Berkman taking the gun from him. "And that's the Frick that the Frick Museum in New York is named after. All that great art!" I felt like applauding him. Stern talked also at length about the poet William Stafford, whom he admired. Then he told me a wonderful story about his years in Switzerland, where he and the poet Jack Gilbert traveled back and forth between Switzerland and France illegally trading in small bits of currency. These are the only ones I remember from an afternoon of stories and commentary and singing and kissing the leaves and staring at the sun. Being with Gerald Stern was like being inside one of his poems, like being folded among the book of his poems I carried with me for weeks. Sober and volatile, surprising and keenly and sweetly alive, he's a direct descendant of Whitman if ever there was one, but more animated, more traumatized, lovesick with life.

Knoxville, November 1989

> A skirt of flames
> dances around her
> at dusk . . .
>   "You and I Are Disappearing"
>   Yusef Komunyakaa

> Uncoiled the steel cable
> From its oily scrotum
>   "The Whistle"
>   Yusef Komunyakaa

I began to read Yusef Komunyakaa as I was considering graduate school and looking for a poet master to work with. In *Dien Cai Dau*, I found the image above from "You and I Are Disappearing" both confounding and mesmerizing. The "skirt of flames," evoking a flamenco dancer in colorful dress, offered itself as a place I could grasp in the poem, though visibility of the flames becomes blurry in the flame-like light of dusk. Another blurry clarity appears in the lines "A tiger under a rainbow / at nightfall," recalling Rousseau's painting "Sleeping Beauty," which I happened to have hanging near my desk. Made up wholly of similes, the poem offers different emotional responses from the poet who wishes to distance himself from the experience. The "girl [is] still burning" inside the speaker's head.

While the poem is ostensibly about the sight of the burning, in fact it's about the cry the girl releases into the air, which the speaker cannot escape. "The cry I bring down from the hills / belongs to a girl still burning / inside my head," he had told us in the first three lines. Did the speaker actually see her burn? Did he only hear her cry and imagined the burning in many different ways? Is the cry even a real cry? We can't be quite sure of the reality of the incident. Komunyakaa's technique of precision and obfuscation, of directness and indirectness where objects become subjects, and vice versa, are meant to unfold a tumultuous psychic truth, where cause and effect are pummeling each other for primacy, as would be the case in a guilty conscience.

I'd noticed this technique in Komunyakaa's later work, especially in the poem "The Whistle," which I read in a magazine before it appeared in his book *Magic City*. The first few lines arrest us with their choice of diction: "The seven o'clock whistle / Made the morning air fulvous / With a metallic syncopation, / A key to a door in the sky—opening / & closing flesh." I had to look up "fulvous" and all the earth tones and references to birds it contains. There's synesthesia with the sound of the whistle changing the color of the air with its metallic beat, and then this metallic sound becomes a key to the sky cleaving, waking, and shaping human lives. Of course, that is what a factory whistle does to its workers and their families, but through Komunyakaa's metaphor, the object and people's experience with it begin to develop a darkly magical association.

I should say that I also knew the town Komunyakaa was writing about. Bogalusa, Louisiana, is the city of his birth, a town on the Pearl River in southeast Louisiana, which I had to drive through in my years of high school as I drove on the weekend back and forth to my brother's apartment in Hattiesburg, Mississippi. Bogalusa had a lumber mill that made the town stink horribly, and in the dozens of times I drove through its empty main road on Friday and Sunday afternoons, I always wondered how people managed to live there. I never stopped to find out, but years later, here was the poem to explain Bogalusa's drabness and the source of its unpleasant feel and smell.

The lumber mill and its whistle dominated nature and the sound itself became naturalized. We read that a winch releases a steel cable from its "oily scrotum," and a rip saw throttles logs, while "iron teeth bit into pine" as "Yellow forklifts darted." It would all seem natural were it not for the humans subsumed in the machinery and if the setting were not so relentlessly grotesque.

The animism Komunyakaa applies to the machinery makes everything slip into legend. Again, metaphor and anthropomorphism provide a psychological explanation.

> The one o'clock bleat
> Burned sweat & salt into afternoon . . .
> Wild geese moved like a wedge
> Between sky and sagebrush,
> As Daddy pulled a cable
> To the edge of the millpond
> & sleepwalked cypress logs.

The whistle is now a bleat with magical powers, burning sweat and salt into the weather. Wild geese, like a blade, cut through the landscape, and the speaker's father "sleepwalk[s]" logs. The "logs" are the object of the sentence, but a reversal of subject and object is suggested. The economy of the wild geese line is simply astounding. It covers so much landscape and severs heavens from earth, creating a foreboding image that intimates the events to come later in the poem.

Somewhere through my readings of Komunyakaa's poetry, an image of Matthew Arnold stuck into my head. In it Arnold, as the master canonizer of the nineteenth century, holds poems like x-rays, measuring them against Milton's light and determining if they're up to snuff. For me, in terms of language and imagery, Komunyakaa's "The Whistle" has been a mirror against which I hold my poems to measure them for the density of effect (keeping adjectives to a minimum, eliminating adverbs and multisyllabic words, keeping the poem muscular with nouns and verbs, listening to the cadence of the words). In "The Whistle," it's all there in exemplary fashion. The poet throws all he knows of language into the service of the poem. The scenes he's deeply imagined are chiseled into taut sound, motions are reconsidered from all angles, and the ideas he wishes to convey are embodied into what the senses can grasp. Joseph Conrad once wrote that his task is "to make you see." Yusef, as a teacher and by example, seems to say "make me see to see."

Knoxville, February 1990

> through your destruction
> i stand up
> "miss rosie"
> Lucille Clifton

Lucille Clifton's work seems to bear a double legacy: Langston Hughes's portraiture and the austere minimalist poetics of the haiku. But there's no proof that either influenced her. In her practice, everything can be said briefly, and the poems are not cryptic or obscure. They say what they're after quickly and clearly; their implications rise exponentially with re-reading. Clifton seems to say, "I'm going to say this once and only once." The oracle does not repeat or elaborate.

Clifton's "miss rosie," who is wrapped in rags and reeking of an awful smell and who used to be the town's beauty, is redeemed by the poet's desire to stand up through that site of destruction. She is redeemed, as she is detested. The poem "cutting greens" celebrates a taste in the poet's "natural appetite" that moves from an "obscene embrace" to "the bond of live things everywhere." The poet wins this moment out of an unwanted encounter—a moment that lacks any strong associations with history until the work of the knife and the symbols of struggle force open a revelation. The poem stops right there, never saying more, never ever dipping into sentimentality despite the powerful emotional transitions experienced by the speaker.

Clifton gives the world a cold-eye, noting her own culpability. In "the lost baby poem," the poet speaker addresses a fetus she aborted while on its way "to meet the waters under the sea." Clifton borrows from Hayden's "Those Winter Sundays," ending the first stanza with "what did I know . . . / what did I know . . ." And like

Hayden, she lays the ground for both self-accusation and justification. She concludes with promises and a curse on herself if she were to "be less than a mountain" for the aborted fetus's brothers. Other poems confront religion, God, and the poet's father and other fathers who knew how to dance but did not know how to "walk like men." The confrontations, sometimes tinged with self-deprecation, unfold into celebration. Other poems take on odd subject matter but end in triumphant and comic notes. In "poem to my uterus," the poet addresses her uterus, which is about to be surgically removed as "old girl" who is "patient / as a sock." Both phrases are apt, outlandish, and tender. In "if I stand in my window," the poet speaker stands naked in her house pressing her breasts against the window glass, confronting "the man" who, offended, wants to stop her. In defiance, she persists until "the man" is forced to discover his true self and to suffer the consequence of his discovery. The scene starts off as farcical but turns serious, suggesting defiant celebration, even of the taboo, as a response to the deadly madness of racism and sexism.

Clifton's prose memoir that concludes her book *Good Woman* tells us a little bit about how her unique voice developed. She's a Dahomy woman, she tells us, identifying the West African tribe as her ancestry. And she was the first to go to college among her extended family in Buffalo, New York. They and she knew that she was a poet at an early age, even though when she got admitted into college, they could not tell the difference between Howard and Harvard Universities. To some degree, this explains her brevity. Like the 'alam poets in my native Libya who worked in an a short oral lyric form, Clifton wanted to "speak" her poems to her community, to make sure that their perception is engaged constantly, that there is no waste of time or language. The poems needed to be heard more than once to make them sink in, but first they must make ear-sense; they must captivate and please with their import, wit and empathy. She does not take her readers for granted, and she's intent on capturing their attention and rewarding them for it. The oral roots of her poems should not deceive us, however. Hers are modern poems with a highly developed use of enjambment and typeface. Empathetic and deeply dignified, they seem to trust the reader to understand them. Her work remains endlessly rewarding to me. Whenever I've attempted a short poem, it's bound to be an homage to her, who had set the bar so sublimely high.

Knoxville, April 1990

> Sundays too my father got up early
> and put his clothes on in the blueblack
> cold,
>
> "Those Winter Sundays"
> Robert Hayden

For two years, I scribbled the closing couplet of Hayden's poem on almost every surface I saw, especially a little blackboard at a coffee shop I used to frequent in Bloomington, Indiana, and repeatedly on napkins while daydreaming. The couplet was like an amulet inside me, something I carried without thinking but that lit me up when I reflected on it. The young Hayden himself became a sort of legend in my imagination, a sensitive, near-sighted young man who could also be resilient making his way through the chronic angers that poverty ignited within his family and world. His father (who as we know was not his "real" father, but Hayden did not know that until years later) remains an enduring image of decency for me. "What did I know?" I repeated the poem's rhetorical question to myself, never ceasing to marvel at the phrase "austere and lonely offices" that ended the poem, my father never far from mind at that time. By the 1980s, he'd wanted me to consider returning to Libya even though I did not want to, and as it turned out, it was still not safe to return. In 1991, I joined him in Egypt as he went through a protracted illness. My desire to be of service was natural, also my wish to make up for my absence and seeming ingratitude. My father too was a silent man. We lived comfortably in my childhood, but from what I gathered from his life, I knew that he began to man a store at the age of eleven, that he had to spend the nights there for almost twenty years to protect the meager goods of that tiny store. This was in the Nile Delta to where my family had immigrated in the mid-1920s, a 1500-kilometer trek that took them months to make and where my father was born somewhere in the Sahara. Despite the comfort we lived in compared to the Haydens, a memory of poverty haunted my father, and his uncomfortable alertness hovered around us. The line "No one ever thanked him" in Hayden's poem rang true, as well as, never enough and no one really knew how. And now that he has passed, I can only utter the couplet to the presence of his absence. Hayden's poem is there with me when that feeling arises. The answer to the rhetorical question at the end of the poem is always, "I know very little about love's austere and lonely offices" and it stings.

What makes the poem remarkable is how Hayden lines up the evidence against himself to deliver the final devastating question. I've taught the poem over the years as a great example of the rhetoric of poetry, of how poetry too must convince us with facts and ideas, not simply deliver emotion. Two years ago, I taught the poem to a group of students (mostly women) at the University of Tripoli in Libya. Their English was adequate, but we had to work through the poem's more demanding images, such as "blueblack cold," and "cracked hands that ached / from labor in the weekday weather made." The students recognized the sternness of fathers and the chronic angers of family life. We worked together to reassemble our sense of the Haydens' poverty, their wood house creaking as it warmed. I'd feared that the power of the image of the father polishing the speaker's "good shoes" would be lost on them, who owned dozens of shoes, but they got it. The final couplet and its "austere and lonely offices" was the hardest part. I could see that some of the women were beginning to tear up, and I myself, despite having known how to shield myself from the poem's power when I taught it. Trying to transfer to them what the poem meant (not what it meant to me), I was nonetheless losing my grip. At some point, I had no more to say. It seemed significant to feel this among my people, a people who after four decades of repression and volatility had no means of expressing shared emotions. Hayden's poem settled among us and silenced us into a meaningful communion.

This so to say that I've always felt a deep sense of gratitude for the poem, how it girded me with its legend. The legend of the poem's content and the legend of how Hayden wrote it, how difficult it was to write and how it panged him, and how he managed to do so with great compunction and tact, creating a cathartic and endlessly affecting drama. Providing a kind of anchor, the poem allowed me to feel centered despite my driftings and failings. And though I still have no adequate answer to its final question, I see the damage as clearly as the potential for repair.

Bloomington, 1990

> Exact resemblance to exact
> resemblance the
> exact resemblance as exact as a

>   resemblance, exactly as resembling,
>   exactly resembling, exactly in
>   resemblance exactly a resemblance,
>   exactly and resemblance. For this
>   is so.
>   Because.
>
>   "If I Told Him:
>   A Completed Portrait of Picasso"
>   Gertrude Stein

I did not read Stein's poem in a book but heard it on a cassette on a long road trip and replayed it several times, fascinated by the inimitable manner it found its way to its astounding ending: "Let me recite what history teaches. History teaches." Stein performs the poem with a commanding voice. She is a strong, rich and polyglot woman of the late nineteenth century, giving a forceful speech, the tone so self-assured that it must be the reader's fault if he did not understand what she was saying. In that way, Stein was reminiscent of the eighth-century Arab poet, Abu Tammam, who when asked, "Why do you write what cannot be understood?" responded saying, "Why do you not understand what is written?"

There are several things going on in the poem, many of which are centered on the words "presently" and "exactly." The painter has to try to be exact and can only capture the present moment of her subject. But before that, she has to get over a hurdle. Napoleon appears and he's hard to dislodge from the poem. The poet sees a resemblance between Picasso and Napoleon[1] and hence has to ask, "Would Napoleon [Picasso] like it?" Would he like her portrait? Without an answer, she goes to render him in a cubist manner, which complicates things considerably. Like paint, which knows nothing of what it is portraying, Stein's words do not name or describe, they are mere sounds like brush strokes of color dabbed on the canvas of our hearing.

Stein slices language in many ways and dices our perception with the desire/illusion of wholeness. In the passage quoted above, she focuses on two central phrases of the poem, "exact" and "resemble," brings them forth as verbs and nouns and adjectives, then binds them with the connective issue of "and," "as" and "in." We begin to sense the infinite as these two words begin to attach in seemingly endless ways. The process takes us back to the origins of speech and creates a distrust of accepted thought and conventions. The more exact and present the painter wants her subject to be, the more fleeting he seems.

Reading Stein's poem, my tongue gets stuck in repetition, and I end up misreading the words or read them in reverse as if Stein induces a sort of dyslexia. Snippets of air or song escape through cracks of our conscious mind. Words or sentences detach themselves from their meanings and recognize themselves mirrored and echoed in other sounds. One does not read words; it's one mouth that begins to juggle them freely.

The words rattle on, but the music is at a satisfactory level. Stein, who loves the iambic foot, in other poems gives us sentences or fragments that resemble each other grammatically or metrically repeats them. These experiments with highly syncopated sounds often end with an anticlimactic sequence of unstressed syllables, or a flat image, a whimper after a whole lot of bang, perhaps so that we read again and linger at the great passage. She goes on, combining words and creating musical patterns by letting phrases circle each other, stomping their stresses at one another.

In this poem, sufficiently hypnotized or enthralled by Stein's drum solo, we receive the final line, which is a perfect iambic hexameter, "Let me recite what history teaches. History teaches." The joy of the poem is in discerning how she got to this end. Listened to or read, the poem presents threads of connection that weave together and unravel repeatedly. In the manner of Stein's best pieces, here cities rise and fall in our dreams. The point is not to enter the cities but to dream them. It's a dream woven of cadence that circles back in ephemeral waves of meaning. This is what Stein teaches.

Bloomington, October 1990

> I know you are reading this poem be-
> cause there is nothing else
> left to read
> there where you have landed, stripped
> as you are.
>
> "Dedications"
> Adrienne Rich

> I choose to love   this time   for once
> with all my intelligence.
>
> "Splitting"
> Adrienne Rich

Even before I became interested in poetry, Adrienne Rich's name had come up, often as a branch, or brand, of feminism somewhat obscured by Gloria Steinem and the NOW movement, but clearly seen as the most articulate. In the earliest poetry chatter I heard, she was supposedly the one who kicked men out of her readings (which turned out to be untrue). To me this legend was even more reason to admire her for giving poetry that impression of tenacity. Reading her poems in anthologies, I admired "Aunt Jennifer's Tigers" for its command of meter and rhyme, and the masterful way the poet had set up an objective correlative for Aunt Jennifer's predicament and quiet rebellion, both expressed by the tigers that "prance across the screen." The terms used, "Aunt" and "Uncle," as well as the setting and the strong current of sorrow and anger below them, reminded me of Ibsen in their quaintness and austerity. I learned later that Rich was in fact an avid reader of Ibsen in her youth.

"Diving into the Wreck" struck me at first as taking on too much or lacking context. But the poem had a degree of passion and a sense of collective responsibility that seemed rare in American poetry. It was also clear that this was criticism coming from within the establishment, a testament of someone who had been expected to belong to the system and was refusing to do so.

"Splittings" added a new dimension to my sense of her work. The formal lilt remains—I mean the somewhat formal bearing and the insistence on poise, but the vulnerability, self-interrogation and longing are unmatched. Addressing a lover with whom she shares a history of suffering, the poet is "fighting the temptation to make a career of pain." The love of another woman has healed her through self-discovery. And even as the lovers are separating, and as love burns and disappoints, the experience seems to enhance her love of life. The poem is simply one of the best love poems ever written.

At the end of a poetry workshop in August 1991 led by Philip Levine, he pulled his reviewer's copy of *Atlas of the Difficult World* and read with great conviction and admiration the final section of the poem "Dedications" to our group I turned to a fellow immigrant poet and found that we were both grinning with glee at Rich's recognition of us. This time too, the mention of the intifada was something I could point to specifically as a nod to me as a reader. Clearly, there was a world to explore, and I set out to know about it in her book, *The Fact of a Doorframe*. There, I found this wonderful passage from the foreword to the book:

> The poems in this book were written by a woman growing up and living in the fatherland of the U.S. of North America. One task for the nineteen- or twenty-year-old poet who writes the earliest poems here was to learn that she was neither unique nor universal, but a person in history, a woman and not a man, a white and also Jewish inheritor of a particular Western consciousness, from the making of which most women have been excluded. The learning of poetic craft was much easier than knowing what to do with it—with the powers, temptations, privileges, potential deceptions, and two-edged weapons of language.
>
> I have never had much belief in the idea of the poet as someone of special sensitivity or spiritual insight, who rightfully lives above and off from the ordinary general life. In writing poetry I have known both keen happiness and the worst fear—that the walls cannot be broken down, that these words will fail to enter another soul. Over the years it has seemed to me just that—the desire to be heard, to resound in another's soul—that is the impulse behind writing poems, for me. Increasingly this has meant hearing and listening to others, taking into myself the languages of experience different from my own—whether in written words, or the rush and ebb of broken but stubborn conversations. I have been changed, my poems have changed, through this process and it continues.

This is as inspirational as any artist statement I could find, and Rich delivers on all of these points and more in her book.

Rich's poems from her first two books work through crises in her personal life as well as her vision of herself as a poet, the two concerns tightly intertwined. A line in her second book, *The Diamond Cutters*, says "My debt is paid. The rest is on your head" thus anticipating a shift that would come eight years later in *Snapshots of A Daughter-in-Law*. Though the title of *Snapshots* ties the poet to her role as wife and positions her under the hegemony of her husband's family (her daughterhood continuing well into her womanhood), the poems declare a search for width and independence. Her speculations regarding the institution of marriage become more confrontational. We begin also to see her placing her experience in a historical context, and also peopling her poems with persona poems and poems addressed to fellow poets, as well as intelligent and humorous critiques such as in "Ghost of a Chance."

Her embrace of free verse in *The Necessities of Life* occurred as

Rich was becoming more radicalized. The title poem has her "reenter the world" piece by piece. She had been "wolfed almost to shreds" and "swallowed . . . like Jonah." This is perhaps in reference to the highly negative reaction to *Snapshots*. But the poet now states, "I learned to make myself / unappetizing . . ." She will "let nothing use [her]" as she "dare[s] to inhabit the world" again. This re-entry into the world moves with anticipatory energy and receptiveness. The poet has "invitations" to houses that are impatiently "waiting" to tell her "their tales." The personal (i.e., apolitical) lyric as it has been defined by the New Criticism has proved too small a stage for all the issues Rich wanted to address. Her poetry becomes dialogical in the full sense of the word as she also takes on the task of being a cultural excavator, bringing to light heretofore unknown facets of women's history. *Leaflets* (1969) includes a poem set in in 1860s, a poem addressed to a Russian poet, a translation of a poem from Yiddish, and a powerful lyric addressed to the poet Richard Howard. I found these transformations illuminating regarding what it takes to be a poet, and they made me look forward to such changes in my own work and career.

One of the most striking poems in *Leaflets* is "Ghazals: Homage to Ghalib," which seems to me to have ignited a shift in Rich's writing process. Rich had worked on Ghalib with Aijaz Ahmed, who had chosen thirty-seven ghazals to be retranslated by American poets, Rich being one of them. As such, Ghalib's ghazals were utterly unconnected. As a translator, Rich, aware of the turbulent context of Ghalib's poems, became familiar with the power of poetic disunity, where non sequitur passages begin to slowly create a world of emotion and meditation. In her own ghazals, this approach allows Rich to gather many of her themes under one roof, rather than tackling each on its own, forming a tapestry of concerns and seeing them all laid out before her. The form allows her to change tone, note facts and images, experiment with pithiness and paradox. We note how she incorporates the motif of oblivion and disappearance into ecstasy, a Sufi motif that would have been readily available to Ghalib. Rather than offering a sense of cosmic irony these devices help her craft crystalline observations earned in duress. The ghazal becomes a kind of diamond, a pressure-induced poetic observation of the world.

Furthermore, Rich's work was a sort a paradigmatic realignment for me. Reading her work altogether and seeing it evolve made me aware of her ambitious poetic vision, a project that aims at confronting the absenting and erasure of women and other disadvantaged groups, fueled by her conscious "refusal to be a victim" (261). Her work emphasizes women's stories and the presence of the female body at work, in love and in nature. There is earthly solidity in the poems, a confidence about the body, an awareness of woundedness, but no special fragility. In making femaleness normative, she demands that such experiences be heard, anticipating also that the masculine imagination cannot fathom not being the center of attention or the locus of pity. In "Meditation for a Savage Child" a young woman rises to address a distinguished doctor at the end of his lecture. She says:

> You have the power
> In your hands, you control our lives—
> Why do you want our pity too.
>   (183)

One can imagine the lecture as being typical of masculine discourse toward women seeking admiration, love, and pity. Once these needs are fulfilled, women are ignored. Rich wishes to challenge this dynamic while also exploring opportunities for dialogue, empathy, and intimacy among women.

"Meditation for a Savage Child" is in *Diving into the Wreck*. Reading the title poem along with the rest of the collection it made much more sense. By then, it was clear that Rich was exploring patriarchy as manifested in American imperialist capitalism and the wreck it has made of the world. Written during the Vietnam war, the poems address the war itself and also probe the paradigms that perpetuate masculine violence against women and the powerless in the world. Feminism in Rich's handling becomes an expansive tool for understanding the nature of cruelty and the possibilities for empathy and repair. It extends the radius of her concerns from the women in her circle to those around the world, to imprisoned writers and dissidents, and reaches further to issues of nuclear weapons, racism, pollution, surveillance and state violence.

Feminism seems also to have widened Rich's sense of poetry and its audience. The poet reaches out, finds new passions and concerns, imagines other writing, engages in dialogues with other poets and friends, and imagines the unsaid. The fact that Rich engages politics directly does not allow her to lose sight of her commitment to the lyric. Hers are personal poems that address vulnerability, longings, and sadness, allowing for the inner life to deepen alongside her social awareness. Love here is the laboratory of the soul where our experience of love and our capacity for it, even as we are wounded by it, enhance our awareness of human potential. Rich in that sense is like the ancient Arab poets who had to begin their poems with their vulnerability—their having loved and lost—without which no credibility can be given to a poet.

The years after *Atlas of the Difficult World* would see Rich continue her mission of attention aided by formal reinvention. Her poetry constitutes the most ambitious and inclusive American poetic projects of the second half of the twentieth century. A master artist, she was, in her lifetime, the conscience of her nation and her language, and a poet to admire and emulate for decades to come.

Bloomington, November 1990

> And this is I a woman alone
> at the threshold of a cold season
> "Let Us Believe in the Coming of the Cold Season"
> Forugh Farrokhzad

Forugh Farrokhzad fell into my hands just as the first American Gulf War was about to start. I read her poems in *A Lonely Woman*, a biography of her by Michael Hillman. The life and the poems came together, but even the biographer could not explain the brilliance of the posthumously published poems, the departure in tone, technique and poetic ambition that Farrokhzad achieves in them.

Everything about Farrokhzad's life seemed familiar as the details were similar to many other stories of Middle Eastern women writers and artists seeking independence and warding off criticism in a conservative culture. The arranged marriage at sixteen, followed by a quick divorce, then famous love affairs, all of these were the stuff of the gossip magazines I read as a boy, along with the sports sections in the newspapers. Familiar too were poems like "Wedding Band," with its obvious use of symbol to critique the institution of marriage. I could swear that I knew a poem like it in Arabic.

Any sense of familiarity with Farrokhzad's work, however, changed once I reached her late poems. "The walnut sapling / is now tall enough to explain the meaning of the wall," she writes in a poem titled "Window." Her sentences are longer in these poems, and the relations she creates between the elements are wild, ecstatic, and heartbreaking. The gaps between thoughts are also larger. Hillman tells us that at the age of twenty-seven (!), Farrokhzad was already feeling that her life had been a waste, because she felt she had not learned enough. This was around the time her remarkable short documentary "The House Is Black" was released in 1963. A highly stylized portrait of a leper colony, the film served as a metaphor for Iranian society as Farrokhzad saw it as an unhealthy, repressive society. The lepers in the film stare directly at the camera, and sometimes speak, both individually and as a group. Lively with humor and rage and melancholy, they express indictment rather than illicit pity. The running commentary is pure poetry, as is the film itself.

It makes sense that Farrokhzad's poetry changed after making the film. Her late, longish poems zoom in and out of family portraits to larger social conditions, rendering the poet's speaker's animated pessimism about it all. The poem "Let Us Believe in the Cold Season" was one I could not shake off for a long time.

> I am cold, and it would appear
> that I will never be warm again.
> I am cold and I know
> that nothing will be left
> of all the red dreams of one wild poppy
> but a few drops of blood . . .
> Time passed
> time passed and night fell
> over the acacia's naked limbs,
> night slithered on the other side
> of the window panes
> and with its cold tongue
> sucked in the remains of the departing day . . .
> How loving you were
> when you carried me to love's meadows
> through an oppressive darkness
> until that whirling smoke, the last gasp
> of fiery thirst, settled down
> upon the field of sleep.

None of this doubtful happiness is going to happen again, not for some time. Toward the end, the poet recognizes a possibility that "green shoots of light" will burst through "the never-ending snow."

But it is an invitation to believe in the beginning of the cold season, a call for resignation perhaps but also a eulogy for a once vibrant embrace of life. Many readers in Iran at the time saw the poem as a sort of suicide note, especially as Farrokhzad died in a car accident shortly after writing it. But the poem does something else. The resignation never smothers the passionate force of life; the elegy/eulogy never manages to convince us, or the poet for that matter, that her life is finished. Farrokhzad's work radiated this vibrancy in the face of melancholy and her late poetry, in its operatic expansiveness was as wrenching as it was affirming.

Bloomington, February 1991

> with black eyes and the look
> difficult to figure—
> "Sand Nigger"
> Lawrence Joseph

> How strange I was, with impure
> thoughts,
> brown skin obsessions.
> You could tell by the way I walked
> I possessed a lot of soul,
> you could tell by the I talked
> I didn't know when to stop.
> "Curriculum Vitae"
> Lawrence Joseph

Reading contemporary Arab poets and translating them for practice, I wrote somewhere else in this book, helped me legitimate my voice with ripples and echoes of their translated words. I learned now to say it right, knowing that there was always more than one way of doing so, some I'd yet to think up. But what to speak of now that one has become an American of sorts? And really what kind of American does one want to be? "Arab American" was the term, and it seemed an awkward combination of words.

I'm speaking about *Grape Leaves: A Century of Arab-American Poetry*, the anthology edited by Greg Orfalea and Sharif Al-Musa. Those were the questions posed by that anthology to me in the early 1990s. And there were many answers. I knew the Mahjar poets, the ones who wrote mostly in Arabic and to the Arab world in the first three decades of the twentieth century. On these shores, Kahlil Gibran's romanticism, highly influential in the Arab world in the early decades of the twentieth century, sounded like a watered down version of Blake's. The few translations of Elia Abu Madhi lacked the melodic effects of his existentialist verse in Arabic. Several voices, however, stood out to me in the anthology: Etel Adnan for her experimental verve, Samuel Hazo for his American poise and Naomi Shihab Nye for her great skill at finding bonds everywhere she went with forgiving irony and conversation. Nye's unassuming sense of wonder allowed her to be a praise singer of humanity, a position few could not assume with any degree of conviction and that I was glad to find among my kin.

Then there was Lawrence Joseph. Hailing from Detroit, his terrain was similar to Philip Levine's but covering a more neglected margin and with a deeper sense of time. The voice in Joseph's poems mixes outrage and distance and afraid to embrace the accusations and presumptions placed upon it. Joseph's poem, "Curriculum Vitae," has an epigraph by Wallace Stevens: "Identity/is the vanishing point of resemblance." The weight of Stevens is obvious on Joseph's second books, but the issues are more urgent. Still abstract—not the abstractness of transcendence—the poems explore how the political economy of capitalism operates God-like, where the sum is much, much larger than the parts. "What Has Become of the Question of 'I' / are topics of discussion / at the Institute for Political Economy," writes Joseph.

In American poetry, private, personal knowledge is poetry's sacred realm. Such prescription can only discourage the poet from imagining the lives of others, many of whom are like him. This Dickinsonian choice goes against the other half of the American grain when we consider how many are gathered in Whitman's' song of himself. Can't poetry gather people also to look upon their condition, and must all be counted individually when the illnesses, obstacles, injustices, and deprivations were experienced collectively? Why can't poetry talk about all of us, us as a global economy when, in fact, that is what we are? Is speaking privately the only way to confront the fact that we are abstracted, our desires reduced to clusters of zip codes, gender, age groups, ethnicities, and income? This is where Lawrence Joseph was a great revelation. It was exhilarating to find a poet who understood Marx's labor theory of value and who did not shy from confronting the demeaning abstractions of capital.

Joseph, it seemed to me, reshaped his identity (Arab Maronite Christian Catholic) into an advantage. Hailing from an ancient Christian community, he forcefully occupies the moral high ground amidst the racism and exploitation that American Christianity has legitimated. Condemning and probing American greed and violence, Joseph stands like an ancient apostle, reminding us that the Bible was written by dark-skinned believers who would not be fooled by justifications of conquest or injustice in the name of morality and national security.

For me, an immigrant from an Arab country, the question of identity was not cultural as much as it was political and philosophical. With Joseph and Edward Said as examples, to be an Arab American provided an opportunity to occupy a particular critical position not limited to seeking scraps in the American political body politic, but to speak from a humanist standpoint shaped by grievance, humiliation, and anti-imperialism, and also by a deep awareness of music, the sad, sad music that makes every Arab tremble, the lute, the flute, and voice that weeps while eyes remain fixed in a defiant stare. To be a poet was to feel out and feel the surge of courage flowing in one's veins. Joseph assures us, it's there, in us and before our eyes.

Bloomington, June 1991

> I might advert
> To numerous accidents in flood or field,
> Quarry or moor, mid' the winter snows,
> Distresses and disasters, tragic facts
> Of rural history, that impressed my mind
> With images to which the following years
> Far other feelings were attached—with forms
> That yet exist with independent life,
> And, like their archetypes, know no decay.
>
> William Wordsworth
> "The Two-Part Prelude"

In the beginning of "The Two-Part Prelude" (an earlier version of the great poem), I was struck by Wordsworth's address to the river Derwent—"For this didst thou, / O Derwent . . . / Make ceaseless music that composed my thoughts," he writes. The apostrophe reminded me of modern Arab poems addressing the Nile and Euphrates that I'd read in my youth. It was not a move that I'd seen in English poetry prior and loved seeing it. Also, in Wordsworth's poem, there's the practice of implied imagery that perhaps relies too much on the reader. "And when the deed was done," he writes without explaining what that specific deed was exactly. I found such imperiousness charming.

The Prelude (all of it) fascinated me because its story resembles that of Ibn Khaldun's *Al-Muqaddimah* (Ibn Khaldun's *Prologomena*). Ibn Khaldun (1332–1406), an Arab historian from Tunisia began working on *Al-Muqaddimah* in 1377 as the introductory chapter to a history of the world, the *Kitab al-'Ibar* ("Book of Lessons"). Meant to explicate the developments of the history of the Arabs and Berbers in North Africa, the *Al-Muqaddimah* became an independent work on its own, known now as the first work of sociology as such. Similarly, Wordsworth began working on *The Prelude* as part of a long poem (three times as long as Milton's *Paradise Lost*, he wrote somewhere), titled *The Recluse*, which he planned to co-author with his friend Samuel Coleridge. The two poets never worked together after the *Lyrical Ballads*, and Wordsworth, who only referred to *The Prelude* as "the poem" or "the poem on the growth of my own mind," worked on it throughout his life. Mary Wordsworth, the poet's widow, published the poem shortly after his death in 1850 under the title *The Prelude or, Growth of a Poet's Mind; An Autobiographical Poem*. I like the idea of *The Prelude* and *Al-Muqadimmah* being ends in themselves. They tell us that to begin one must be ready to tell everything.

The Prelude seems to me an attempt to capture moods that are running ahead of the poet. I get this feeling most from reading "The Two-Part Prelude," which contains versions of the two first two books of the great poem and where Wordsworth is at his fastest pace, exhilarated by the beginning. Wordsworth, of course, is well known for his definition of poetry as "emotion recollected in tranquility." The word "recollected" is essential, for while it also suggests some authorial control over the subject described, there's also a sense of belatedness. The poet is belatedly recollecting an intense emotion from the past. And we as readers are belatedly reconstructing through the poet's work an emotion that is being chased after.

All of this creates rungs of distance that inevitably place the original emotion, which is not poetry but the life origin of the poem, at a higher level than the poem.

In "I Wandered Lonely as a Cloud," Wordsworth explains how emotion and recollection work. Seeing "A host, of golden daffodils / . . . dancing in the breeze" the poet could not help "but be gay" in the "jocund" company of the spring flowers. This event flashes upon the poet's "inward eye" when he's at home in a "vacant . . . or pensive mood," and fills him with pleasure. The recollection gives the poet a jolt of joy in the midst of ordinary life. Wordsworth attempts to make the recollection (or the poem) more significant than the event itself. "I gazed—and gazed—but little thought / What wealth the show to me had brought," he writes, suggesting that the wealth did not come until later, in the act of recollection. But even as we read the poem, we note that the energy was in the event (the poet is standing, the flowers are dancing in the breeze), not in the recollection while the poet is lying on his couch.

Reading "The Two-Part Prelude," I felt that Wordsworth wanted to take on the poem's belated relationship with experience and to give poetry the upper hand. The poet keeps pulling and pulling at memory, adding incidents and interpretations as if to insist that the poem can contain them, that it is greater than its incidents and the act of their recollection. At one point, he confesses that he began to tell his story aware of "The weakness of a human love for days / Disowned by memory." Clearly, the poet fears nostalgia, things that memory disowns and imagination enlarges and distorts. It's also possible that we want to reclaim what memory has no control over. In either case, the poet undertakes the act of recollection to "fetch / Reproaches from [his] former years, whose power / May spur me on." I love the phrase "fetch reproaches," as if the poet wants to recollect from his past stories that will grate at him with guilt so that he could do better in life. In some ways, that is the job of the poem, too, that is, to interrogate the past and to make of its parts a greater whole.

Reading some of the footnotes provided by the editors, one couldn't fail to notice how much Wordsworth actually addressed in the poem. We know the name of the drowned man whose clothes young Wordsworth saw piled on a lake shore one afternoon, also the name of his servant, and the date of his father's death. Wordsworth mined everything. The scholars also tell us that he was wrong about some facts, and that he lumped facts into a kind of fiction. As to the emotions recollected in tranquility, it seems clear that Wordsworth also recollected emotions he may not have had. He himself notes that emotions and events are transformed with "Far other feelings" that attach to them and begin to exist "with independent life." Our "imaginative power" has "a fructifying virtue" that "nourishes" and "repairs" the important incidents of our lives.

Guided with a notion of child psychology influenced by Coleridge's ideas, Wordsworth wants his poem to address everything, the facts of his childhood and their implications. Through his frequent use of apostrophe, water and the clouds and the wind are all animated. Even ideas (essences, he calls them) walk beside him singing, groaning, or breathing softly. And as he recounts incidents that he did not know much about, he pauses to tells us where it is that his imagination is filling the gaps. As such, autobiography is not mere recollection but an assignment of values to certain moments and a meditation on how personal experience can become a transport to the psychological and universal. In "The Two Part Prelude," which is a beginning of a beginning to a great book that was not written, I found a poem vital with energy, and through it, I saw a poet driven by a great rhythmic engine, madly striving to make his poem greater than the sum of his life.

Cairo, September 1991

> And if you cannot make your life as you want it,
> at least try this:
> "As Much as You Can"
> Constantine Cavafy
> Tr. Edmund Keeley, and Philip Sherrad and George Savidis

I read Cavafy in Cairo when I spent a year there. His poetry permeated me and for months a sober, droning voice hummed inside me. With all trickery and adornment removed, Cavafy's take on life seemed like a solid substance one could lean on. I can't account for the prosody (whether he used rhyme and meter or not), but in Norman Keeley and Philip Sherrad's hands, the poems in English had a sculptural presence. Auden's interest in Cavafy made sense to me as Cavafy in free verse provided an explanation for what bothered me about Auden's adorned classicism. The Cavafy drone, his steady knowing timbre, settled into me. The world takes away our loved ones by death and other means, and we end up mourning them in our poems. It eats up our time and does nothing to address our propensity to ruin our lives.

Cavafy lays bare our limitations, admits to the hopes and notes the discrepancy because we all have to live in it. We have to also live with the regret of our wasted encounters. Then there is the writing of Ptolemaic history, which Cavafy discusses as if he was living in Alexandria then. Indeed, the Ptolemaic period was Classical Greece's last hurrah and witnessed the usurpation of the Greek world within the Roman one. Picking up where the Ptolemaic chronicler Synesius (373–414 AD) left off, Cavafy is not surprised by any aspect of human folly, especially the decadence and hypocrisy of the Greeks as they slowly surrendered to Rome.

At first I was irked by the fact that the Alexandria of the late nineteenth and twentieth century, the Alexandria of my parents, meant so little to Cavafy and hardly appeared in his poems. Cavafy had drawn a portrait of a world I knew, or thought I knew, and he did not offer a way to glimpse anything familiar in it. But with time, I understood that Cavafy may have seen himself as a sort of colonial subject, an elevated local informant, who saw his status as a cog in the British empire similar in many ways to that of his ancestors who were subsumed by Rome. History was repeating itself in a fashion, and he wanted to account for the discrepancies to understand his era. It should be noted that Cavafy gave up his British citizenship after the British bombed Alexandria, not Athens or Constantinople. He was an Alexandrian through and through and by choice.

Most importantly to me, Cavafy was a wonderful entry into the magic of classicism in the sense that his contemporary and Pound's friend, T. E. Hulme, spoke of,[2] where beauty lay in perfect forms, and in this case the form of sufficiency, the form of not overdoing and not presuming. Cavafy expresses no flights of fancy or excessive hopes, no escape from reality. In fact, betrayals and bad luck abound in his poems. The god abandons Anthony after granting him much success and joy. Ulysses' arrival to Ithaka will likely be disappointing, he tells the great hero. In both cases, one has to remain steadfast. The poet tells Anthony, as the great general contemplates suicide, to "go firmly to the window / and listen with deep emotion." He tells Ulysses to curb his disappointment when he arrives in Ithaka and to be thankful to his city for the quest she had given him. Don't be greedy, don't whine at your loss after so much success and joy, be grateful for what you have achieved. As such, Cavafy is a deeply moral poet, in the manner of the ancient Greek lyric poets, who also preached steadfastness and bucking up. But what gall the poet has! Imagine telling Ulysses and Anthony the hard facts of life and placing oneself as a kind of sage, or even a God, telling the hero—humbled by circumstance how he should deal with his turn of fortune. Constantine Cavafy, the clerk who hardly progressed in the world of business living in lowly Alexandria, an agricultural port on one of the edges of the empire, stands as judge and counselor to the greats.

And then there are Cavafy's erotic poems that burn with longing and despair. They are not love poems per se; the lovers don't know each other and engage in illicit homosexual encounters that never grow beyond that. As heartbreaking and brief as these moments are, they give the lovers solace as the imagination shines in them with fantasy, and the spirit which has grown to dismiss so much about humankind is now receptive and hopeful. Those who do not take these opportunities while they have the chance will grow to regret them. Only in the erotic realm does Cavafy tell us to seize the day, even as his carpe diem is tinged with melancholy and bears a hint of death, too. In fact, one does not leave Cavafy's poems urged to take up any action—except perhaps to never let go of the pleasures of the body. Cavafy certainly did but in a manner that sickened him with guilt.

This last biographical element complicates Cavafy's vision but deepens the timbre of his lyrical wisdom. That year in Cairo, away from the confessionalist and post-confessionalist thicket of American poetry, it was refreshing to encounter a poet who did not need to be healed and who had no wish to transcend life. Cavafy had made a complicated peace with the truth. I did not want to, could not, let go of his grasp.

Cairo, January, 1992

> I wander all night in my vision,
> Stepping with light feet . . . swiftly and
>   noiselessly stepping
>   and stopping,
> Bending with open eyes over the shut
>   eyes of sleepers;
>   Walt Whitman
>   "The Sleepers"

Whitman, in the anthologies I read when I started out, tended to give a loud version of himself. "Captain, My Captain" was extremely loud. The lilac by the dooryard bloomed loudly and melodramatically. After these loud encounters, I put him aside for years, anticipating a man to man at some point. Later, reading the 1855 edition of *Leaves of Grass*, I encountered "The Sleepers," and have been encountering it ever since. It seemed to me that Whitman was up to something different in this poem. Unlike himself elsewhere, he begins hesitantly with light feet wandering inside his vision at night. It's an obscure setting and his are the only open eyes in the room. He proceeds to give us his best human catalog, where he, without saying it, seems to bless all the sleepers, the lovers, male and female, the old and young, the murderer and the murdered, all in the democratic state of sleep. And having slept beside them, "each in turn," he begins to "dream all the dreams of the other dreamers / And I become the other dreamers." The poet then launches into his more exuberant self, and he becomes the multitudes occupying their trepidations and desires. At one point, he is the dead person underground, meditating upon his past life.

The shift between the parts is not quite smooth, but one gets used to this with Whitman. A scene of a swimmer fighting the waves begins, and the poet addresses the waves crushing him to death. Then he watches a ship sinking and feels deeply helpless. And of course, the ubiquitous Whitman helps "pick up the dead and lay them in rows in a barn." Another section narrates a scene from the Revolutionary War, the defeat at Brooklyn, and Washington kissing his soldiers on the cheek.

The sixth section gives a personal reminiscence of a Native American woman who showed up one day at the Whitman homestead. Whitman's mother "had no work to give her, but she gave her / remembrance and fondness." The passage goes on:

> The red squaw staid all the forenoon, and toward the middle of
>   the afternoon she went away,
> O my mother was loth to have her go away,
> All the week she thought of her, she watch'd for her many a
>   month,
> She remember'd her many a winter and many a summer,
> But the red squaw never came nor was heard of there again.

The above passage reminded me of my mother and how she dealt with the many semi-strangers that knocked on our door seeking work and kinship. Those were encounters of sisterhood, where friendship and joined labor became the basis of sharing one's abundance. The concept here is *sadaqah* (which is the root word for charity, friendship and truth telling). In the passage above, we find Whitman at his most gentle, most personal. One loves Whitman for his larger self, not for the truth of his autobiographical self, but here he's touched with loss and tender sadness. One can even say he's a bit shy, and I love it.

Soon enough, he grasps energy from thin air. "A contact of something unseen—an amour of the light and air," he writes and begins to describe a scene of homecomings, all sorts of strangers finding their way home. A new catalog launches forth, and the sleepers, the swimmer, and shipwrecked sailors are also accounted for. They are "averaged" and "restored" by sleep. The rest of the poem is a laying on of hands, but where people converge and contradictions fuse into oneness. The nightly procession soothes the poet but also sends him into subtle melancholy. He promises to return. "I will duly pass the day O my mother, and duly return to you." "Mother" here stands for a multiplicity of meanings, including, death, life and lover.

How do the various parts add up? I've never been able to come up with an answer. I'm certain, however, that the poem is greater than it parts, as is the case with Whitman often. I keenly remember my joy in the poem's utter freedom of structure and how the poet moved from topic to topic following his symphonic instinct. The poem answered many questions about the modern long poem, especially about poetic intuition and how to gain authority through it. In this case, it is all in the opening scene with its multitude of sleepers, and the poet's presence among them transporting us from identification to forgiveness. Whitman's "Sleepers" provides no steps to be followed as to how that transport could take place, but he encourages an intuitive approach in seeking it, in persisting in seeking it.

Cairo, April 1992

> The bright melody drowned
> the salvos from the ghetto wall,
> "Campo dei Fiori"
> Czesław Miłosz

What do memory and culpability have in common? That was the question Miłosz's "Campo dei Fiori" posed to me. The poet is in

Warsaw during the storming of the Warsaw ghetto, and his mind drifts to a square in Rome where the Catholic Church burned the astronomer and philosopher Giordano Bruno for being a heretic. Bruno contested the church's core beliefs, including the trinity, the virgin birth and the divinity of Christ and his miracles. He was also being punished for proposing that the stars were distant suns orbited by their own planets and that the universe was infinite and had no center.

The poet imagines the square and the sumptuous plenty of its market, with merchants selling olives, lemons, fish, wine and flowers. He describes how Bruno was burned and how the spectators went back to their business as soon as they could. The poet then turns to the scene before him in Warsaw in 1943, where the city's non-Jewish population enjoyed a beautiful spring day. The music of a carousel drowns out the sounds of the Nazi salvos pummeling the ghetto. And though people did see black smoke rising from there, they went about their business as if nothing was happening.

The poet has several choices now; first is to condemn both the people of his city and the people of Rome, and "the oblivion / born before the flames have died." But he decides instead to focus on the loneliness of the victims, and how they've found no words for the people who lived on to explain their negligence, which also points to the poet, too. The victims are devastated by the betrayal of their fellow citizens. Miłosz concludes the poem with a complicated idea: there will be other Campo de Fioris he tells us, and the dying and the lonely always will be forgotten. But there is some use in us still. Our tongues will become an alien language that will speak for the victims, when rage "kindles a poet's words."

I did not quite understand the poem's ending then and find it unsatisfying now. Poets will be the ones who resuscitate that suffering and will bring back the memory of the victims. The victim's deaths will not be in vain as long as the poets remember it, and they will, Miłosz assures us. But that seems like a consolation that rewards the poet, even hinting that the suffering took place so that rage sparks his creativity. It's a bit conceited, youthfully so perhaps. It's also true; victims are ignored, and the only genuine way they are remembered is through poetry, a personal kind of poetry. We are that cruel and unkind, and only poetry can document our cruelty and attest to the existence of our conscience at the same time.

What excited me about the poem then, and still does now, is the historical parallel Miłosz makes between Bruno and the

Warsaw ghetto fighters, positioning them both as truth tellers. Time and history do not change the criminality of the apathetic; they are witnesses, too, of the dead weight that we feel inside our hearts. In its claiming of two different and distant atrocities, the poem means that we need to respond to all the suffering we witness or know of, with hand or word, or by the heart (which is the weakest sign of life, as Muhammad tells us), for our own suffering to be dignified.

Bloomington, December 1992

> These are roads to take when you think
> of your country
> and interested bring down the maps
> again
> "The Book of the Dead"
> Muriel Rukeyser

I came to Rukeyser's poem after examining the work of experimental poets, who exhibited social awareness and political ambition but who wrote simply uninviting texts. Flat language and half-digested abstractions vied with easy irony and stand-up comedy. In that sense, Rukeyser's poem was the poem I wanted to read but could not find for quite some time. Offering a traumatized American landscape with echoes of Zola, the poem thrilled me with its experimentation, advocacy, and substance. "The Book of the Dead" was also rich with musical phrasing and poetic command. The poet's politics did not weaken her grip on the lyric. Also, Rukeyser never lets go of her sense of wonder at science and the natural world—her lines on hydrodynamics are quite astounding. She introduces different voices and timbres that make the poem move briskly, raising its cinematic effect to epic. The poet was always a step ahead of us. Ending each poem/scene, she surges to a new one, and we move from the lyric dizziness of one section, expressing shock, dismay, disappointment, or sorrow to another. The different sections sound out different rhythms, some slow and thick, others such as the quotes from the Congressional hearings that resemble call-and-response chants. The poet does not allow the material to write itself, and it was material that could have indeed written itself.

The beginning of the first section is a powerful invitation, an act of claiming and citizenship. Here, "poetry" is speaking and tells the cosmopolitan New York poet to take the road into her country, to which she has yet to belong. Poetry also tells the poet, these are the roads to take when you think of your country. Belonging lies in the moving inward into your country, in the friction of coming and going across it. It is the road that will tie "you to its meaning."

"The Book of the Dead" provides a great map for the long poem, a much more coherent map than, say, "The Waste Land." The requirement of the epic being a poem about history, or with history, as Pound says, is quickly fulfilled. In the second section, the poet takes you through West Virginia's history, where the poem's main story takes place. Two quick cinematic swoops, and we witness the tragic death of miners in West Virginia, who died due to Union Carbide's greed and neglect. What the rest of the poem does is an amazing example of poise; it tells a story that needs to be told and delivers on the esthetic mission that needs to be fulfilled. Rukeyser brings us to philosophy via the lyric to engage the future and offers no escape route from responsibility through cosmic irony or religion.

As I started writing this memoir, I came across criticism stating that Rukeyser did not make it clear that the victims in the Hawk's Nest Tunnel disaster were mainly black, that their death was a racist and an economic crime. Perhaps she assumed we would know that, with several sections that deal with race. Or as a leftist artist, she may have wanted readers to recognize the workers as workers, not so much their race. Or perhaps it was a tactical, political decision so that issues of class and exploitation are given primacy over race. We know now that such suppression in the long run does not work. The American working class was racially divided during Rukeyser's time and remains so. Do I feel cheated because we/I did not think of the workers' race even though Rukeyser refers to some black workers? Is the poem marred by this discovery? No and no. The poem remains a great example of how an artist can strike a balance between ethics and esthetics, a poised stance between political expediency and artistic dignity.

Bloomington, March 1993

> It was autumn. Beyond each village the wind
> Threw gusts of yellowing leaves across the road.
> "The Widening Spell of Leaves"
> Larry Levis

I renamed Levis's book "The Widening Spell of Levis," soon after my friend the poet Talvikki Ansel gave it to me. The poems exemplified pure poetry as Walter Benjamin had defined it and seemed to reverse the notion of poetic creativity as the ancient Arabs understood it. I'm talking about spells. For Benjamin, the poem (actually the translation) flickered with the existence of something pure and magical; for the Arabs, the poem came to the poet when a spirit took hold of him. Levis seemed a possessed poet pointing to a spot in the distance and trying to take us there.

Levis's sentences loop, extend, change tone, give chase to a thought, stop to smoke a cigarette midway and stare at the camera and talk. There's an American, youthful showmanship about the angst he presents. The same mind that has discovered that "It's all or nothing in this life; it's smallpox, quicklime, and fire," refuses to give up on beauty. We embrace beauty to fight the ugliness of the world, neither one is going away. Kindness and violence stand together, and in Levis's pace, we meander between them, often taking the turn toward praise. We cannot escape our inner life or the interplay between recollection, self-interrogation, and wonder, where irony intervenes often. "The Tree so old it has outlived even its life as a cliché," he writes. A Brechtian magician; Levis wants you to be mesmerized while also making fun of the show.

The title poem of the book has the speaker driving from Skopje, the capital of Macedonia, where stands a two-thirds scale replica of the "Arc de Triomph stuck / in the midst of traffic and obstructing it." The speaker is ill and lost, driving without a map until the road suddenly comes to an end. The symbolism of this particular journey, so far from the poet's home, a journey in an absurd place, can easily stand for the poet's life. But there was much else going on in the poem. The poet crowds his poem with others, the villagers who do not respond to his queries, villages that became poorer as he drove on, and "the herds of goats / And cattle, the spiraling leaves . . ." Soon all that company fades, and even the road disappears. Despite his illness, he wishes to investigate the silence, the non-resolution and the end of human agency. Now he's a Sufi in a state of *fanaa* (oblivion), in order to "feel the spreading stillness of the place/Moving . . ."

Narrative does not suffice; the poet simply cannot end the poem. He seeks memory for a pattern and recalls an experience of disappearance. The poem brings up a childhood memory (or a fiction) of Japanese American neighbors who disappeared for weeks during the internment of Japanese Americans during World War II. The poet recalls all that he could of his connection with Mr. Hirata, the photographer, all that disappearance meant to him as a child. The poet hallucinates about Mr. Hirata in a Macedonian landscape that widened to encompass the nature of all spells. The two narratives do not connect or inform each other. They only share the yellow leaves that were "Nothing except their little reassurance / Of persisting." One story unfinished opens into another, and one story finishing and claiming the cosmos of its explanation. Neither of these are successful narrative strategies, but we soon realize that is not what Levis is after. We are in the thralls of a poet in the thralls of giving meaning and stripping it and reapplying it again to an unexplainable world, a world that "couldn't be / *Compared* to anything else, not even the sleep / of some asylum at a wood's edge with the sound / Of a pond's spillway beside."

Levis offers the consolation that our sorrows are marked and that emblems of them will resound "until the end of time," in the hope that his meditation could be felt again, and that his spirit's labor lingers and penetrates. The textures of his exposition, the sentences that build ideas and unbuild them, present his poems like architecture rising in the landscape. And while his poems enact the fragmentation and futility of language, Levis does the avant-garde, rather than merely meta-write it. Mournfulness over the loss of language and its incapacity to connect us permeate his poems, as if he's aware that he is writing on water, that his thought-story will be absorbed again into the shapelessness of language. Reading him, we watch a philosophical dance that we can neither imitate nor that the poet can perform again. It's a spell that happens to both reader and poet at the same time. Reading Levis, I understood why I always detested the phrase, "the poet uses poetry . . ." It is clear that Levis did not use poetry, but poetry used him, as he gave her as good as she took. May that be our fate as well.

Notes

1. Picasso did, in fact, remind Stein of Napoleon.
2. Hulme, T. E. "Romanticism and Classicism." http://www.poetryfoundation.org/learning/essay/238694